SAMPLERS

SHIRE PUBLICATIONS

Dear Rosa oh, what ails this heart
Sure tis of stone, it cannot smart
Nor yet relent the death of thee
Whose death alone could ransom me

M. A. RENDELL. Oct. 20. 1835

SAMPLERS

REBECCA SCOTT

SHIRE PUBLICATIONS

Published in Great Britain in 2009 by Shire Publications Ltd, Midland House, West Way, Botley, Oxford OX2 0PH, United Kingdom.

44-02 23rd St, Suite 219, Long Island City, NY 11101, USA.

E-mail: shire@shirebooks.co.uk   .

www.shirebooks.co.uk

© 2009 Rebecca Scott.

All rights reserved. Apart from any fair dealing for the purpose of private study, research, criticism or review, as permitted under the Copyright, Designs and Patents Act, 1988, no part of this publication may be reproduced, stored in a retrieval system, or transmitted in any form or by any means, electronic, electrical, chemical, mechanical, optical, photocopying, recording or otherwise, without the prior written permission of the copyright owner. Enquiries should be addressed to the Publishers.

Every attempt has been made by the Publishers to secure the appropriate permissions for materials reproduced in this book. If there has been any oversight we will be happy to rectify the situation and a written submission should be made to the Publishers.

A CIP catalogue record for this book is available from the British Library.

Shire Collections no. 2   .   ISBN: 978 0 74780 706 3

Rebecca Scott has asserted her right under the Copyright, Designs and Patents Act, 1998, to be identified as the author of this book.

Designed by Tony Trustcott Designs, West Sussex, UK and typeset in Bembo.

Printed in Malta by Gutenberg Press Ltd.

09 10 11 12 13   10 9 8 7 6 5 4 3 2 1

COVER IMAGE

Sampler by Mary Hope, aged 10 years old, dated 1801. Private collection. Photograph courtesy of Witney Antiques.

PAGE 2 IMAGE

This sampler, worked by M. A. Rendell in 1836, is strongly influenced by the developing fashion for Berlin needlework which was to sweep Britain and America in the nineteenth century.

ACKNOWLEDGEMENTS

I owe a huge debt of thanks for their enthusiasm and friendship to a great many people, regrettably too numerous to mention individually, who have shared their knowledge, insight and expertise with me. I must, however, make special mention of a few individuals without whom this book would certainly not have been possible: firstly, my mother, Joy Jarrett, for all her painstaking research over the last eighteen years; Justin and Stephen Jarrett, for their photography; and David Hewitt and Martin Ellis, for their help with the illustrations for this publication. Without the work of many individual historians far less would be understood about samplers and their history. Carol Humphrey, Kathleen Staples, Betty Ring, Edwina Ehrman, Naomi Tarrant and Linda Eaton all deserve special mention. I would also like to thank Carol and Stephen Huber, Mr and Mrs Arnold, and Witney Antiques for the provision of the illustrations used in this publication. Thanks are also due to those at Robert Scott's for giving up their office space, and for their computer expertise, especially Carly, Kelly and Gary.

CONTENTS

A B C D E F G H I J K L M N O P Q R S T U V W
X Y Z abcdefghijklmno pqrstuvwxyz

1 2 3 4 5 6 7 8 9 10 11 12 13 14 15

REBECCA SCOTT NOVEMBER · 1 · 1790

Two things, the needle and the book we find,
Help to accomplish all the female kind,
The shineing needle draws the fine spun thre
Bedecks the person and adorns the head,
Since neatness gives the charm that all commend,
The needle is the female choicest friend,

PREFACE

THE history of sampler making has enjoyed a considerable and growing fascination from the mid twentieth century onwards, by those introduced to the subject through a love of stitching, and by those who are curious about the lives of the children and families of a bygone era. Samplers provide a decorative and visually stimulating history of both stitching and pattern, and the values and teaching practices of the last four hundred years. The accessibility of museum and gallery collections and the publication of a number of new books and original research have encouraged a change in the way we now look at samplers. No longer are they regarded as the insignificant toils of childhood, but they are increasingly recognised not just for their decorative appeal but also as important historical documents. It is hoped that by having some understanding of the historical and social context in which these samplers were worked the reader will enjoy a greater appreciation of these fascinating, poignant and often charming works.

From the earliest known dated sampler, worked in 1598, to the early part of the twentieth century samplers were generally worked by children, and although there are exceptions, it is usually with childhood that samplers are associated. The fact that samplers can sometimes provide the only surviving record of lives that would otherwise remain undocumented, and were often regarded as unimportant, makes them a valuable tool in understanding the attitudes towards the upbringing and education of the children of the past.

With the advent of the twentieth century, and the fundamental changes that the First World War and growing industrialisation and modernisation were to impose upon society as a whole, the necessity for domestically produced clothes and household textiles waned. Throughout the developed world women were achieving greater political equality and educational opportunity than they had previously known and the working of samplers by children in schools gradually ceased. Instead the working of samplers has developed largely into a recreational interest or hobby taken up by adult women. The existence of a plethora of clubs, guilds, societies, and publications that have evolved to educate and cater for the interest of the modern adult needle worker in either reproducing or creating their own original 'sampler' is one reason why the history of the sampler and its development in the twentieth century are only briefly mentioned in this publication and not examined in any detail.

Opposite: Signed and dated 'Rebecca Scott November 1 1790', the verse on this sampler makes explicit the importance of needlework skills in eighteenth-century society.

INTRODUCTION

WHEN one mentions the word 'sampler' many of us conjure up images of young girls meticulously working rows of cross stitch alphabets and numerals, occasionally embellishing them with carefully learnt moral verse or the occasional house or potted plant. Whilst these samplers are amongst the most commonly found today, the history of sampler making is a complex one that goes back several hundred years and crosses both geographical and social boundaries. Wherever and whenever embroidery has been an important, necessary, or popular aspect of the decorative arts – for domestic furnishing, costume and clothing, state, military or ecclesiastical embellishment, or simply as a social accomplishment – it is likely that samplers have been worked.

'Sampler' is derived from the Latin word *exemplum*, meaning an example or model to be followed, and it would seem probable that ever since man has worked cloth with embroidered designs samplers have been used for recording and practising different patterns and stitches. The very earliest surviving examples are thought to date from AD 400 and were worked by the ancient Peruvian Nazca culture.

During the last years of the nineteenth century and the early part of the twentieth century there was a growing interest in excavating ancient archaeological sites, particularly those in Egypt, and amongst the items found in the tombs were decorated textile fragments, thought to date from AD 400–500. Subsequently several well-known classicists of the time left large collections to museums and thus several have Mamluk samplers amongst their collections, some believed to date from the fifteenth century, and perhaps even earlier.

Whilst this demonstrates that man was embroidering cloth and recording patterns on cloth in North Africa and South America at this time, we have no firm evidence to tell us when the first samplers were worked in Europe: as yet no samplers have been discovered dated prior to 1598, although there is documentary evidence of samplers being worked from the earliest years of the sixteenth century, and it seems highly probable that samplers were worked earlier even than this.

One of the earliest surviving documents recording a sampler is that in the household accounts of Queen Elizabeth of York (1465–1503), now preserved in the Public Records Office, which contains the entry: 'To Thomas Fissch, for an elne, of lynnyn cloth for a sampler for the Quene, viijd.'[1] In the will of Margaret Thompson of Freston-in-Holland, Lincolnshire, dated 25 May 1546, there is a clause which states, 'I gyve to Alys Pynchebeck my sawmpler with semes'.[2]

Samplers are also mentioned in literature of the period, perhaps the best-known being in Shakespeare's *A Midsummer Night's Dream* (Act III Scene ii):

> *Helena:*
> We, Hermia, like two artificial gods,
> Have with our needles created both a flower,
> Both on one sampler, sitting on one cushion

Following the invention of the Gutenberg printing press in Germany around 1450, the ability to print spread rapidly around Europe, with William Caxton producing the first English printed books at his press in Westminster in 1477. Before this date, in the western world, books were generally hand copied and therefore rare; most often produced by the religious orders within monasteries, they were usually confined to religious subjects. Printed pattern sources did not exist for a needle worker to follow prior to this date so therefore it would seem probable that in the absence of printed material samplers were worked out of a necessity to record both the stitches and the patterns used on the wide variety of embroidered textiles produced, whether amateur or professional. Once established, the use and production of printed patterns in needlework design spread quickly throughout Europe and by the end of the sixteenth century the use of samplers solely as a reference tool was no longer strictly necessary.

Samplers were, however, to become a most useful tool in the education of young females. They were used to teach not just the different stitch techniques necessary for marking and mending household linen, but provided an occupation which banished idleness, inculcated the young embroiderer with morals and obedience, and taught schoolroom lessons. They were also to provide a useful method of recording all manner of information from births, deaths and marriages to household accounts and even musical scores.

It is of course from this period that the earliest dated samplers are found, and perhaps the reason for the survival of samplers from this date is not merely coincidental. For it is just as their sole function as a work tool diminishes and their importance as an educational aid becomes a reason for their production that we see samplers survive in any great numbers. It seems logical that the reasons for the survival of samplers from the last years of the sixteenth century and throughout the seventeenth century are firstly that they did not wear out from repeated handling through use, and secondly that they were regarded as treasured possessions, records of a young girl's accomplishment, handed down from one generation to the next.

Chapter One

THE SEVENTEENTH CENTURY

THE earliest dated British sampler, now in the collection of the Victoria and Albert Museum in London, was completed in 1598 by Jane Bostocke and dedicated to her first cousin once removed, Alice Lee. The sampler includes two dates, the first being the date of Alice's birth (1596) and the second the date the sampler was completed. The sampler contains a number of rows containing blocks of different border patterns worked in a variety of stitches below the inscription to Alice. Amongst the motifs stitched above the inscription are a deer, a lion, and a talbot (a hunting dog), all family crests of the Lee and Corbett families. Traces of family crests pertaining to Jane's branch of the family have been unpicked. Possibly Jane unpicked her family crests when she gave Alice the sampler although it is not possible to know for certain. After its discovery in the 1960s it was assumed that Jane would have worked the sampler at a relatively young age; however, from recent study it has become clear that Jane worked the sampler in her adult years and not as a child.[3]

Of course the changes in sampler usage and subsequent design did not happen suddenly but took place over the course of several generations and quite probably at different rates in different parts of Europe. But it is none the less from the early years of the seventeenth century that samplers survive, and it is to this century that we must first look if we are to understand their importance in documenting the social, political and religious changes in society – or even if we simply wish to appreciate their appeal as objects in their own right.

The seventeenth century was undoubtedly one of great political and social change. The century that saw the monarchy removed and then restored, two civil wars and the early foundation of a parliamentary system of government was also the century that saw perhaps the greatest flourishing of amateur domestic embroidery. Think of the complex intricate raised work caskets, pictures and mirror frames, or the minutely worked tent stitch pictures and cushion covers. Samplers were an integral part of this tradition of embroidery.

It is useful to consider the role of needlework in seventeenth-century society as a background to understanding the importance of samplers. Firstly, when looking at written documentary evidence such as letters and books it is important to understand seventeenth-century terminology. Today embroidery and needlework are often used to describe the same activity, but in the seventeenth century they were used to describe two distinct practices. Needlework usually refers to work carried out on an open weave plain linen foundation cloth (often referred to at the time as a canvas). The usual choice of threads for such work was either a wool yarn, often referred to as crewel, or a silk floss thread. Typically needlework stitches were

Opposite: Detail from a seventeenth-century spot motif sampler showing the inclusion of small insects and a bird worked in between the geometric and floral motifs.

This typical English mid-seventeenth-century raised work embroidered picture is worked with silk threads on a silk satin ground, and incorporates a variety of semi-precious stones, glass beads, and coral.

tent and cross stitch, and the work produced could range from large-scale bed hangings to small purses or sweetmeat bags. The use of metal threads on tent stitch work is also found as a decorative element. Embroidery was a term used to describe work on a finer, more costly ground fabric such as silk satin or velvet, and often decorative materials such as seed pearls, spangles, precious and semi-precious stones were incorporated into the body of the work. A far greater range of different stitch techniques was employed in embroidery, and these pieces were sometimes embellished with applied decoration, or with raised and padded designs.

In addition to understanding the differences between embroidery and needlework, it is important to understand that when in contemporary accounts a woman is referred to as 'working' it means that she was specifically engaged with her needle.[4] It may be, however, that the work she was engaged in might have had a more utilitarian function such as mending or marking household linen or articles of clothing.

The time spent 'working' by the females in seventeenth-century households would have been substantial, and it engaged women from throughout the social spectrum. The production of all manner of household furnishings, items of clothing, accessories, devotional items, gifts, as well as on occasion items to sell, would have

A finely worked tent stitch pillow cover dating from the mid seventeenth century. The scenes depicted on the pillow tell the story of Esther's petition to her husband King Ahasuerus to save the Jewish people. The Old Testament stories that extol the virtues of being a wise and good wife were popular subjects for needlework and embroidery during the seventeenth century.

Detail from a seventeenth-century raised work embroidered picture depicting the story of King Potiphar. The use of seed pearls, coral and glass beads to embellish embroidery was not uncommon during the seventeenth century.

been undertaken. It is often thought that the working of samplers was simply a preparation for young girls prior to them working items such as the fashionable caskets, mirror frames and tent stitch panels, and that from their samplers they would be able to pick out favoured motifs or border patterns to incorporate into their finished work. From the latest research it would seem that this notion is rather fanciful. Instead, generally the designs for tent stitch panels, mirror frames, caskets, and indeed many other objects were purchased already drawn out on the foundation cloth, ready to embroider.

There has been much conjecture as to the precise nature of the pattern drawers and how and where they worked. In the light of very recent research it would seem that the pattern drawers worked within a workshop system, and were often working either directly or in close association with professional embroiderers.[5] The subjects chosen for these designs were taken from the many printed sources available in the seventeenth century, the most usual subjects being scenes from the Old and New Testaments and the popular herbals and botanicals of the time.

It is interesting to note that many embroidered objects were worked by young girls – in fact from contemporary written accounts and letters many of them far younger than we could imagine possible today. The largest extant group of needlework and embroidery by one individual is that by

Above and right: Detail of a raised work leopard and bird, taken from a seventeenth-century embroidery.
The padding is usually either a plant fibre not unlike kapok, or wool padding – although other materials such as sawdust and even carved wooden blocks were also used.

Martha Edlin (in the collection of the Victoria and Albert Museum in London). The earliest worked of the six pieces was a polychrome band sampler worked when she was eight, her casket being worked when she was just eleven.[6]

The young Hannah Smith tells us in a note found tucked in her casket:

the yere of our Lord being 1657
if euer I haue any thoughts about the time; when I went to Oxford; as It may be I may; when I haue forgoten the time, to sartifi my self; I may Loock in this paper & find it; I went to Oxford; in the yere of 1654, & my being thare; near 2 yeres; for I went in; 1654; & I stayed thare;1655; &I cam away; in 1656; & Iwas almost 12 Yers; of age; when I went; & I mad an end of my cabbinete; at Oxford, & my quenest h; & my cabinet; was mad up; in the yere Of 1656 at London; I haue ritten this; to sartisfi my self; & thos that Shall inquir; about it …

Not only does this tell us Hannah's age, it also clearly tells us that the casket was sent away to London to be made up. Unfortunately Hannah does not give us the name of the person who made up her casket but it appears that her casket was sent to a professional workshop. As yet little documentary evidence either exists or has been found that tells us precisely what kind of workshops were responsible for the making up of these mirrors and caskets. Were they made up by upholsterers or cabinet makers, or by those working within a professional embroidery workshop? In fact many different trades would have been involved in the production of not just a casket such as Hannah's but also the many popular objects created from embroidery and needlework during the seventeenth century. The fact that many different trades were profitably employed in the business of supplying materials and making up the completed needlework bears testament to the popularity of amateur as well as professional needlework in seventeenth-century society.

If needlework and embroidery were an important pastime either as a favoured leisure activity or as a necessity, it played an equally important role in the education of young females. Education – and more particularly female education – had been the subject of much debate from the sixteenth century onwards: the Reformation

Unfinished seventeenth-century tent stitch picture, c.1660, revealing the professionally drawn pattern, which the needleworker then filled in.

meant that direct contact with the scriptures was no longer confined to the clergy and scholars who could read Latin; it was available to all those who could read. Whilst religious leaders vehemently disagreed in their attitudes regarding the role of female education and its place in society, a debate was at least taking place. The Catholic religion, where the focus of worship was within a church, was becoming a less potent force in society, and Puritan values were influencing family structures, with the household increasingly becoming the setting for worship. Whether from necessity or out of a genuine change in society's attitude, the old ideal of a broad classical education, albeit only for the daughters of the rich, seems to have given way to the idea of education for a broader group of women, where scholarly learning was less important than learning to read the scriptures and learning to live a good and moral life.

Bathsua Reginald Makin (*c.*1600–*c.*1675), described as 'England's most learned lady', was known amongst other things for her treatise entitled *An Essay to Revive the Ancient Education of Gentlewomen, in Religion, Manners, Arts & Tongues* (1673). In this essay Makin uses the argument of 'learning as an aid to a moral life, to women's usefulness and moral agency'. Reputed to be versed in many modern languages as well as Greek, Latin, and Hebrew, as well as mathematics and the sciences, she is careful to point out that she does not 'plead for female pre-eminence, [for] to ask too much is the way to be denied all'. Bathsua, who came from a middle-class background, and worked her way up to become tutor to the Princess Elizabeth, daughter of Charles I, whilst advocating female education, suggests that those who should enjoy the fruits of education are the daughters of the wealthy leisured classes, 'persons that God has blessed with the things of this world, that have competent natural parts'. Bathsua writes that the daughters of the wealthy would make the best use of their time 'in gaining arts, and tongues', rather than 'to trifle away so many precious minutes merely to polish their hands and feet, to curl their locks, to dress and trim their bodies'.[7]

It is against the background of social change, where family structures were affected by the political and religious turmoil created by the civil wars and subsequent restoration of the monarchy that we must see the prevailing attitude to female education. How far young females were educated and what type of education they received as previously stated depended very much on their social status. Women of the noble classes and emerging gentry and merchant classes were expected to acquire the social and practical skills necessary for the smooth running of their households, which would include the supervision and production of domestic furnishing textiles. The daughters of the poorer classes would need to acquire the skills necessary to equip them for service in such households.

Central to all female education was the idea that, regardless of background, education should equip the recipient with the female attributes of industry, virtue, and godliness. Books written on the subject of female education recommended needlework to prevent young women from being idle. The working of needlework or embroidery was, aside from being time consuming, an occupation which required neatness, concentration, self-discipline and patience. It seems likely that samplers and their working were used to teach these skills as well as the more functional ones associated with stitching. The incorporation of the decorative bands on seventeenth-century samplers could also have been used to teach the girls the mathematical skills associated with counted thread work and the planning of their designs.

The upper echelons of society tended to educate their daughters within the home, instructed by private tutors; if they had brothers they might receive tuition in a broader range of subjects. The daughters of the middle classes were sometimes sent to live with the families of wealthier relatives to receive their education, or perhaps to one of the 'public' girls' schools, of which there were increasing numbers being founded at this time.[8] Bathsua Makin founded one such school at Tottenham High Cross in or around 1662. The daughters of the poor, if they were fortunate enough to receive any formal education at all, could have attended one of the growing numbers of charity schools.

It seems that samplers were worked both within the household under the direction of either a tutor or family member, and within the school curriculum. The largest group of known seventeenth-century samplers worked under the tutelage of one woman is those worked under the direction of Judith or Juda Hayle, who was teaching in Ipswich some time before 1690. What is not known is whether she was running a school from her own premises or whether she was teaching in the homes of her pupils.[9]

Seventeenth-century samplers generally fall into three distinctive groups: spot motif samplers, polychrome band samplers, and white work samplers. It is, however, quite common to find bands of white work worked on otherwise polychrome band samplers. It is the polychrome band samplers which have survived in by far the greatest numbers, and with which we are most familiar today. To understand why this should be, it is necessary to look at who produced these early samplers and why.

In the early years of the twentieth century when the study and exhibition of samplers was in its infancy it was assumed that spot motif samplers dated from the early years of the seventeenth century. This was perhaps because out of all the surviving forms of sampler it is perhaps easiest to recognise the functionality of spot motif samplers as a record of different patterns to be kept and referred to when needed, and as demonstrations of the different treatments by which any one design could be worked. As we know, the original purpose of samplers was to record stitches and patterns – probably a tool of professional needleworkers in an age before printed patterns existed – so it seemed reasonable to date these to the early years of the seventeenth century. It had also been assumed that the relative scarcity of spot motif samplers also made an early attribution more probable, and the fact that so few are dated meant that it was hard to disprove this theory. Study of the Goodhart Collection of samplers at Montacute House in Somerset has however revealed that of the very few dated spot motif samplers the earliest date recorded is 1640, with the remaining examples dated to later in the century.[10]

Unlike other forms of sampler making from this period, it is notable that with very few exceptions spot motif samplers are not named and do not carry inscriptions. It seems that the most likely explanation for this is that despite the increasing circulation of printed patterns these samplers were intended for the personal use of the embroiderer, to be kept as a record of their favourite motifs; they also allowed the embroiderer to try out the different stitch techniques. In short, this format of sampler was worked for practical reasons whilst at the same time demonstrating the embroiderer's knowledge of traditional designs. It could also be argued that, unlike other samplers worked at this period, the omission of names, dates and inscriptions points to them being worked by adults or professional workers. If this was the case then their repeated use could explain their scarcity.

Spot motif or random sampler dating from the middle of the seventeenth century. Worked in coloured silks on a plain weave linen, many of the motifs incorporate the use of a silver metal thread. The motifs worked on this sampler are both geometric and floral.

Detail taken from a seventeenth-century spot motif or random sampler showing geometric designs worked in coloured silks and metal threads. Many of the geometric designs resemble the parterres so fashionable in grand seventeenth-century gardens.

The most frequently found motifs on spot or random samplers are geometric and floral, occasionally interspersed with insects, butterflies, and animals. Far less frequently found are representations of people or heraldic emblems. It is interesting to note that many of the designs found on spot motif samplers are also found on the many small embroidered objects such as purses, sweetmeat bags and book covers, objects often given as gifts. They also frequently include the use of metal thread, which was often used to enhance the designs found on many of the embroidered objects of the seventeenth century. The sampler shown on this page demonstrates the use of this technique in the majority of the individual motifs.

A close-up detail shows the decorative use of metal threads. It has been suggested that often the floral motifs are placed towards the top of the work above the geometric designs and, whilst this is not always the case, in the majority of known spot motif samplers this is the convention.

The embroidered flowers and plants on these samplers are often taken from

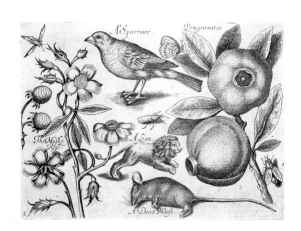

Plate from A Book of Flowers, Fruits, Beastes, Birds and Flies exactly drawne. *Printed and sold by Peter Stent, 1661.*

printed sources, either the herbals or botanicals of the period or pattern books produced especially for the needle worker. Amongst the best-known pattern books, from which numerous sampler designs were worked, was Johann Sibmacher's *Schön Neues Modelbuch*, published in Nuremberg in 1597. By the end of the sixteenth century and throughout the seventeenth century the publication of pattern books was widespread and numerous books were published in England.[11] *The Needle's Excellency*, which reproduced many of the designs from Johann Sibmacher's publication, had by 1640 gone into twelve editions. Richard

Shorleyker's *A Schole-house for the Needle* showed designs including birds, fish, insects and flowers, as well as patterns for lace and other forms of embroidery. Instructions were included with the patterns not only on how to work them but also on how to enlarge or reduce them.

> I would have you know that the use of these squares doth showe, how you may contrive any work, Bird, Beast or Flower: into bigger or lesser proportions according as you shall see the cause.[12]

Title page from A Book of Flowers, Fruits, Beastes, Birds and Flies exactly drawne.

The number of books and individual prints produced in the seventeenth century specifically for needleworkers are too numerous to mention individually by name, but amongst the most influential was *A catalogue of plates and pictures that are printed and sould by Peter Stent dwelling at the Signe of the White Horse in Guilt-spur street betwixt Newgate and Py-corner*, first published in 1660. The designs offered by such publications were not just plants and animals but also emblems and figures. Representations of royal figures were particularly popular, as were biblical characters, notably Adam and Eve.

The designs would have been traced or pricked out from the pattern books on to the ground fabric, a practice which probably accounts for the rarity of surviving pattern books from either the sixteenth or seventeenth century. Those that do survive often show the marks created when the patterns were transferred from book or print to cloth. Herbals and botanicals also provided designs to copy or follow, and the black-and-white illustrations were often easy to reproduce as embroidery patterns. It was often the case that whilst these books were produced primarily as references for students of botany and horticulture their use as references for the embroiderer was not overlooked. As late as the eighteenth century Robert Furber published *The Flower Garden* (1732), which he recommended as 'very Useful, not only for the Curious in gardening but the Prints likewise for Painters, Carvers, Japaners, etc., also for the Ladies, as patterns for working…'.

Whilst the illustrations that appeared in these publications were based on observations taken from nature, and on many embroidered works it is clear that an attempt has been made to replicate this accuracy, the embroiderer would have also been very aware of the allegorical and metaphorical meanings of the plants and flowers she was stitching. In the seventeenth century religion and nature were never far apart. The idea that plants and flowers had innate qualities and virtues was widely held in the seventeenth century, as was the belief that associating with and cultivating these flowers would mean that those same virtues could be transferred to the worker. Contemporary books on horticulture often suggest an association between garden and paradise: by creating one it is possible to achieve the other.[13] Flowers and plants were also seen as symbols of beauty and were associated with the ideas of romantic love. Even today we use the language of flowers and plants to describe female beauty: 'rose-red lips' and 'lily-white skin', for example.

Amongst the most popular flowers and plants that appear on embroidery are the tulip, rose, pansy, violet, cornflower, lily, carnation, honeysuckle, pink, thistle, columbine, marigold, cowslip, strawberry plant, and iris. It is helpful to have an understanding of the meanings of the floral images worked on these samplers because it explains why certain images were chosen for inclusion on all manner of embroidered objects, not just samplers. Seventeenth-century society would have understood these meanings and been able to read a piece of embroidery like a book. It should also be noted that the use of colour was an important consideration: colours also had symbolic meanings, and flowers were one method of depicting these meanings. The language of flowers was used not just in embroidery but throughout Tudor and Stuart society; that the yellow of marigolds was associated with jealousy is in evidence when Chaucer describes Jealousy as 'wreathed in marigolds'. Just as we give flowers today, embroidered gifts were often given in the seventeenth century and were frequently used to convey a message from the giver to the recipient.

The tulip, which appears positioned at the top of the sampler illustrated on this page, was not brought to the West until half-way through the sixteenth century. Originally imported from Turkey, its name comes from the Turkish word for the gauze that was used for their turbans and reflected the shape of the tulip flower. During the sixteenth century tulips were not widely known in Europe and even in the seventeenth century they were cultivated only in the gardens of the very wealthy. They were very expensive and were seen as a mark of social status, and their shape led to them becoming the emblem of the chalice.

The rose had since ancient times been a symbol of earthly love, pride, victory and passion. Greeks and Romans had associated it with their goddesses of love, Aphrodite and Venus, and it had long been used to convey messages of love. The rose in association with the Virgin Mary also came to represent the ideas of heavenly bliss and divine love.

The pansy or heartsease, which appears on many spot motif samplers, was said to be a favourite flower of Elizabeth I, which could account for its popularity on samplers. The pansy was seen to represent the Trinity because it appears to have three faces; its Latin name, *Herba Trinitatis,* reflects this belief. It was also symbolic of chastity, a virtue associated with the Queen. Shakespeare refers to the pansy as 'love-in-idleness': in *A Midsummer Night's Dream* the sap of a pansy was used as the love potion that was rubbed on to Titania's eyes.

The violet has many of the same symbolic meanings as the pansy; indeed the wild pansy is sometimes called the 'Trinity violet'. Differentiating the pansy from the violet in embroidery demonstrates the importance of the use of colour. It is a feature of spot motif or random samplers that

Spot motif or random sampler worked in coloured silks on a linen ground, dating from the mid-seventeenth century. This sampler has retained much of its original colour. The inclusion of butterflies, often recognised as representing the resurrection, is sometimes associated with the restoration of the monarchy in seventeenth-century needlework.

the use of colour is often naturalistic; interestingly, this is frequently not the case on band samplers.

The hanging flower heads of the cowslip (also known as 'herb Peter') were believed to represent the keys of St Peter, whilst the cornflower's popularity as a decorative floral motif comes not only from its bright blue colour but because it was believed to have healing powers. Blue flowers signified faithfulness, fidelity, and peace.

The lily had since Greek times been associated with the throne; it was believed to have sprouted from the milk of Hera, the queen of the gods. Lilies symbolise chastity and virtue and are often seen in painting as a symbol of the Virgin Mary. The lily is sometimes represented in the stylised form of a fleur-de-lis and in fact continued into the nineteenth century as the Prince of Wales' feathers, often seen on the late nineteenth-century samplers worked at the Bristol Orphanage.

Pinks and carnations are amongst the oldest garden plants, and with a history spanning over 2,000 years they are rich with symbolic meaning. Members of the same family, their botanic name, *Dianthus,* comes from combining the Greek word *dios* (divine) with *anthos* (flower). It is believed the carnation's name is derived from the Greek word *corone* (flower garland) or from 'coronation' because of its use in Greek ceremonial crowns. And it is thought that pinks were named either because the jagged edges of their petals looked as though they had been cut by pinking shears, or that their name is derived from the German *pinksten* or *pfingsten*, meaning flowers that bloomed at Whitsuntide. During the sixteenth and seventeenth centuries they were generally referred to as 'gilliflowers' and they came to symbolise a mother's undying love for her child, and the union of the divine and human in the body of Christ.

Honeysuckle was the symbolic flower of enduring faith, and it has been suggested that the origins of the early patterns were derived from the Tree of Life. It had been a favourite flower of the Tudors and appears in literature of the period.

The thistle, which in general appears on samplers dated after the accession of James I, represented the major sins in mythology; however, it seems more likely to have been used as a symbol of patriotism. It is frequently found used in conjunction with the Rose of England after the union of England and Scotland.

The columbine represented the Holy Spirit: its flower head resembles the shape of a dove, which was a recognised symbol of the Holy Spirit.

In Greek mythology the iris is named after the goddess Iris who personified the rainbow and acted as the link between heaven and earth. In seventeenth-century England it was imbued with the same virtues as the lily.

The strawberry plant usually appears in early patterns as both flowering and fruiting at the same time. Popularly associated with perfection, it was sweet without either thorn or stone, and as it grows close to the ground it was safely assumed not to be the fruit of the Tree of Knowledge. Strawberries were popularly cultivated in the gardens of seventeenth-century households.

The anonymous sampler illustrated on page 22 has a wide variety of different images of flowering branches. Amongst their other meanings, these would have been seen as representing the Trinity, which was often represented by three flower

Seventeenth-century spot motif or random sampler. The representations of the animals, birds and insects as well as the floral motifs are taken from one of the books of engraved designs so popular during the seventeenth century.

heads emanating from one branch – often a fully opened flower, a part-opened flower and a bud. The grouping together of three flower heads on one stem or three stems in one pot or vase is used for similar effect. The use of flowering and fruiting branches which combine different varieties is common in seventeenth-century embroidery, just as the art of grafting the fruit of one plant on to the stem of another had become fashionable in horticulture. The images of weird and wonderful plants producing many different flowers and fruits is in evidence on many of the decorative furnishings and accessories with which the Tudors and Stuarts would have been surrounded. The stories of the Creation, Adam and Eve and the Garden of Eden were subjects with which the population would have been very familiar and they were powerfully and frequently translated into decoration.[14]

Birds, animals, and insects are motifs that occur with regularity on spot motif samplers. Originally it was believed that the small motifs, most usually butterflies and insects, were used most often simply to fill in gaps in the ground fabric, but it seems just as likely that they were included as decorative motifs in their own right. Certainly they were advertised in publishers' lists of printed patterns available to the embroiderer, and were popular motifs on embroidered domestic furnishings, accessories and costume of the period. These too had symbolic associations that would have been widely understood by a seventeenth-century audience, the butterfly representing transformation and resurrection, the dragonfly transience, and the ant hard work and attention to the harvest, to name but a few.

The geometric knot patterns on the spot motif samplers are reminiscent of the patterns found on Byzantine, Celtic and Islamic art and some of the same designs are found on early Mamluk samplers, the fleur-de-lis on the diaper pattern being one such example. They are also reminiscent of the knot gardens or parterres so fashionable from the sixteenth century into the seventeenth century. It is interesting that knots are identified with the coats of arms of many well-known Tudor and Stuart families, and it is thought they represented the 'complexity of human relationships to self, other and the physical world'.[15]

When one examines the reverse of spot motif samplers it is possible to see how very skilled the embroiderers were, and it also indicates how bright the original colours were on seventeenth-century work. It is easy nowadays to identify the muted colours of needlework that has faded over several hundred years; however, when these samplers were first worked their colours would have been very strong.

Representation of flora and fauna in embroidery is to be found throughout the seventeenth century – in fact it would be hard to find a piece of embroidery from the period that did not include some flower or plant image. The use of figures, however, on spot or random samplers is far less common, as is the use of heraldic devices.

It is often the case on spot motif samplers that certain of the designs are left unfinished or only partly worked, often revealing the progression of embroidered stages necessary to achieve the finished work. This indicates that these pieces were intended to demonstrate or remind the worker of the necessary stitches and patterns, rather than simply to work them as practice exercises. It also saved on time and the purchase of expensive silks and metal threads.

By far the largest surviving group of samplers worked during the seventeenth century are band samplers. These take their name from the repeated rows or bands of different designs and inscriptions worked across the width of the sampler. The foundation cloth or ground is generally cut from one complete width

Detail taken from a spot motif sampler showing a fleur-de-lis worked in silver metal thread. This motif was popular on both English and continental samplers.

Detail of reverse of a spot motif sampler showing the vibrant colour with which samplers were worked in the seventeenth century.

A rare spot motif or random sampler showing a courting couple dressed in period costume. The inclusion of figures in spot motif samplers is relatively rare.

of a plain weave linen, although examples exist which are worked on a foundation of two joined pieces of linen. The selvages are therefore at the top and bottom of the sampler and the sides then hemmed to provide the required width of the sampler. As a result the shape of the samplers is generally fairly long and narrow. The average length of a sampler is usually between 20 and 25 inches, although samplers are known which are considerably longer (samplers as long as 42 inches are known).[16] Occasionally two equal-length pieces of linen are joined along their long side to form a double sampler, but this is quite rare. It is worth mentioning at this point that occasionally the lack

A detail taken from a spot motif showing a half-finished design. The deliberate part working of motifs is common to many spot samplers.

of a selvage top or bottom of the sampler can indicate that the sampler has been cut subsequent to its making.

The threads used on seventeenth-century English band samplers are almost without exception coloured or white silks. This is perhaps an indication of the social and economic prosperity of the girls who were receiving an education during this period. (Interestingly, at the time of writing no known seventeenth-century samplers can definitely be attributed to a Scottish worker.)[17] The linen ground used for working the samplers was very expensive, which probably accounts for the fact that these samplers are densely worked. The importance of embroidery as part of a young girl's education cannot be over-stressed and a band sampler would in all probability be only one of a number of forms of sampler that would have been worked during the course of her education.

Unlike the spot motif samplers, it is far more common to find band samplers that are initialled or named and dated, although it is still probably true to say that the majority are not. The range and complexity of the stitches employed in the making of these samplers is perhaps why the

Above: This English band sampler worked by Elizabeth Forde in 1658 makes use of expensive, brightly coloured floss silks. When this sampler was worked England was under the protectorate of Oliver Cromwell.

Left: English band sampler initialled 'MC', dating from the mid-seventeenth century. Worked in coloured silks on a linen ground, the sampler is worked primarily in a running and double running stitch.

Above: Detail taken from an anonymous band sampler dating from the mid-seventeenth century, showing the wide variety of stitches found on samplers of this period. Running and double running, chain, stem, satin, and detached buttonhole are amongst the different stitches worked on this sampler.

Right: Seventeenth-century band sampler worked in brightly coloured floss silks on a linen ground. The lack of an inscription is not uncommon on samplers worked during the seventeenth century.

Below: Detail taken from a seventeenth-century English band sampler, showing a floral band featuring acorns, worked in coloured silk on a linen ground.

Opposite far right: Band sampler initialled 'SH' and worked in 1677. In this sampler the 'boxer' figures are clothed, although the outfit is clearly there for modesty rather than to depict period costume with accuracy.

seventeenth century is known as the 'golden age' of sampler making. Amongst the many different stitches commonly found on band samplers are double running, buttonhole, detached buttonhole, chain, satin, cross, Montenegrin cross, rococo, Hungarian, Algerian eye, Russian over cast, plaited braid, French knot, couching, stem, and cushion stitch. It is obvious from almost all seventeenth-century samplers that needle skills were still very much at the heart of their educational value.

The bands contained a wide variety of border patterns, generally one or two repeats of each pattern in each band. The inspiration for the designs came from the same pattern books from which the designs were taken for the spot motif or random samplers, and the geometric and floral subjects were the most common. Acorns and oak leaf, carnation, honeysuckle, rose, lily, cornflower and strawberry patterns formalised and worked into border patterns were amongst the most popular. It is true that just as in the spot samplers the embroiderers would in part have chosen certain motifs because of their symbolic meaning. The anonymous sampler illustrated on page 26 and dating from the mid seventeenth century has no fewer than nine border patterns worked with the acorn motif. The acorn had a symbolic association with Britain for many hundreds of years, and it became associated with the Royalist cause in the seventeenth century after Charles II was believed to have hidden in an oak tree in the grounds of Boscobel House whilst fleeing from the Puritan forces after the Battle of Worcester in 1651.

The representation of small male figures known as 'boxers' is also one of the most popular subjects appearing on band samplers. The figures were given the name 'boxer' because of their stance, usually arranged in pairs, facing each other,

A band sampler worked with a single naked figure of a boxer. In this depiction the lower half of the boxer's body resembles that of an animal and not a human.

appearing to have their arms raised as if they were opponents ready for the fight. They are also usually holding a small object in their outstretched hand. It is actually the case that they are derived from motifs of two cupids or lovers exchanging gifts, which frequently appeared on earlier continental embroidered needlework. On English samplers the female figure has usually been replaced by a tree or a geometric shape that vaguely resembles a bush or flowering plant. The figures appear in various states of dress: the illustrated sampler initialled 'SH' and dated 1677 shows a band of boxers clothed, whilst the boxer in the anonymous sampler is shown naked.

Representations of human figures on band samplers are relatively unusual but do appear increasingly from the second quarter of the seventeenth century. The elaborately dressed women in the sampler initialled 'EI' and dated 1656 are unusual; it was, however, not uncommon for those figures that do exist to be dressed in contemporary costume, with the exception of Adam and Eve, who are usually depicted wearing the customary fig leaf.

Identifying the flowering plants and fruits that appear on band samplers is not always straightforward. Transferring patterns taken from printed sources onto the ground cloth often involved counted thread work and as a result patterns and motifs are often distorted or stylised. The band second from bottom on the anonymous sampler illustrated on page 29 shows what look like pineapple plants, although it is difficult to identify some of the different conical shaped fruits, which include bunches of grapes, pineapples, strawberries, pomegranates with their seeds exposed and artichokes. Where leaves are seen projecting from either side of the fruit it has generally been interpreted as representing a pineapple. During the seventeenth century pineapples were associated with royalty, particularly after Charles II was famously depicted receiving a pineapple from the royal gardener around 1670. Grown in the tropical climate of the East and West Indies, the pineapple became associated with England's prominence as an important trading nation. The New World, from which not only pineapples but many other tropical fruits came, was becoming a source of inspiration for the gardeners responsible for the fashionable gardens of the period, and because of the new and strange flowers and fruit which grew there it was also believed to be the closest place on earth to the Garden of Eden. Pineapples and other fruits not native to England were starting to appear in the gardens of royalty and the very wealthiest households, and in 1669 pineapples were listed amongst the fruits grown in the gardens of Hampton Court.[18]

Far left: A band sampler initialled 'EI' and dated 1656. The centrally placed row of three ladies dressed in contemporary costume is particularly striking. This sampler combines polychrome bands with three rows of white needle lace.

Left: Anonymous band sampler dating from the mid-seventeenth century, worked with eleven rows of stylised flower and plant forms.

29

Detail of a border pattern showing a stylised representation of a pineapple, taken from a seventeenth-century band sampler.

As the seventeenth century progresses the samplers include more indications that they were being worked as classroom exercises, with the inclusion of alphabets and inscriptions becoming more common. The moral verses that are almost ubiquitous on eighteenth-century samplers become increasingly prevalent on later seventeenth-century samplers. The verse on the sampler initialled 'SH' and dated 1679 provides a good example of the sorts of inscription which are most common:

WELL GROWNE IN GRACE
WELL LEARNED AND WELL
TAUGHT BY FAITH AND GOOD
WORKS IS SALVATION
WROUGHT

Opposite right: This complex band sampler dating from the seventeenth century belongs to a related group of samplers of which three others are known. The fifth band featuring the Angel is worked in a technique intended to imitate Assisi work.

Opposite far right: Rare band sampler worked with both polychrome bands and white work panels. The retention of the original parchment is unusual but provides evidence of the embroidery techniques employed in the seventeenth century.

Common to many band samplers is the inclusion of inscriptions or rows of alphabets worked upside down; this may well be the case with border designs as well, but it is far less apparent. It seems that the likely explanation for this is that either the samplers were on occasion worked by more than one girl, each working from opposite ends of the sampler, or that for ease of working or in an attempt to prevent soiling the same girl worked her sampler from both ends.

The sampler illustrated on page 31 (left) shows a technique that attempts to imitate Assisi work, where the background is in-filled and the design is left either wholly or partially unworked. This sampler is one of a group of three samplers that share many of the same designs and are worked using the same techniques. One is in the collection of the Victoria and Albert Museum in London; another is in the Goodhart Collection, housed at Montacute House, a National Trust property

in Somerset, and the third is in a private collection. It is possible that these samplers were worked under the instruction of the same person, although in the absence of more information worked on to any of these samplers it has not been possible to identify an individual teacher, or indeed where they were worked.

Bands of white work embroidery, cut and open work, and pulled thread work are often incorporated into otherwise coloured band samplers. The sampler illustrated on page 31 (right) is particularly interesting as it retains the original parchment that supported its working.

White work samplers required perhaps the greatest skill and concentration levels shown on any form of sampler. The high degree of skill required in their making suggests that these were worked by girls who had already achieved a high level of proficiency in other embroidered tasks. It has been suggested that a white work sampler would likely be the final task of a young girl's education, before she moved on to embroider decorative household accessories such as mirror frames, cushions, and caskets.

They generally consist of either one or a combination of different techniques. The first technique is known as cut or open work: this requires the worker to remove a section of ground cloth by removing both the warp and weft threads or by removing either the warp or weft threads, possibly leaving just a few threads in place to act as a joining between the top and bottom borders of the linen ground. The design was built up by overcasting the raw edges and then working rows of buttonhole stitch, each row worked into the preceding row. Sometimes either vertical, horizontal or diagonal bars were stitched across the open spaces left in the ground fabric to add strength and a framework for the design. The designs were then worked in a variety of different in-filling stitches, including buttonhole, hollie point, and superimposed buttonhole. The designs created using this method resembled the needle lace used on the fashionable costume of the period.

A second technique required the interlacing of threads attached to the overcast stitches forming many small squares, which could then be in-filled to create mainly geometric designs. The decorative effect achieved closely resembles the work popular on table and tray cloths of the nineteenth century. Generally this second technique does not produce such a complex or fine appearance. Drawn thread work is also found on seventeenth-century white work samplers, as are bands of white work embroidery, usually worked in satin and double hem stitch.

The designs for white work samplers were taken from printed pattern sheets and books, in much the same way as they were in coloured band and spot motif samplers. The close-up of the white work band shown on page 35 (top) shows a man and woman dressed in elaborate fashionable costume; the design is based on a pattern published in Sibmacher's *Modelbuch* of 1601. A very similar depiction, clearly taken from the same printed source, is illustrated on page 43 of *Samplers, Fitzwilliam Museum Handbooks* by Carol Humphrey.

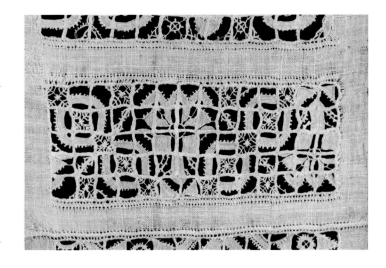

Detail of panel of white work needle lace.

Opposite left: Seventeenth-century white work sampler with multiple panels of needle lace.

Detail of white work needle lace. The rose is worked with detached petals.

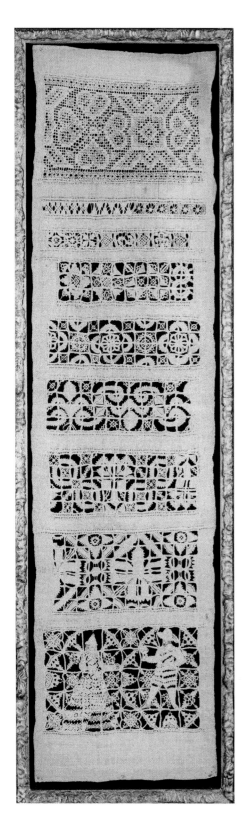

The detail of the sampler illustrated on page 35 (bottom), also depicting a man and woman in the fashionable costume of the period, illustrates a courting scene in which the gentleman is carrying his hawk or hunting bird on his arm whilst the lady is presenting him with a favour as was customary in the seventeenth century. This sampler is worked with many detached elements to the design: the tent sides are flapping open, the costumes are raised away from the ground and the petals of the flowers are detached and raised, giving the design a depth rarely seen on white work samplers of the seventeenth century. The detached pieces were sometimes worked separately and sewn onto the sampler. Raised designs are rarely found on samplers of the seventeenth century and yet raised work embroidery was very popular during the middle and later years of the century. Perhaps the answer lies in the practicality of storage: a sampler with raised designs would be hard to roll up the traditionally accepted method by which these samplers were kept.

White work bands had a practical application, and reflected the fashions of the day. The demand for lace on costume during the seventeenth century was still enormous, and lace edgings for ruffs, collars and cuffs were particularly fashionable. Ruffs required very long lengths of lace for their decoration and so it seems unlikely that it was produced domestically but was instead the product of professional workshops. The working of lace or drawn thread work for smaller projects, however, seems far more likely to have been carried out within the home. Trimmings for christening robes, cuffs, coifs, caps and collars could and would have been attempted by young women in the home. The making of cut and drawn work samplers starts to decline at around the same time as less costly continental lace imports arrive in England in greater quantities around the end of the century.

It has been argued that when considering the samplers of the seventeenth century one should be careful not to over-emphasise the symbolic meanings often attributed to the motifs commonly found on them, and that the choice of pattern and design was influenced by many factors. It seems reasonable to assume that the choice of patterns depended heavily on what printed sources were readily available to the teacher, either in school or within the household. It should also be remembered that it was not uncommon for designs to be transferred from sampler to sampler and

Detail of a figurative panel taken from a white work sampler. The design for the man and woman is based on one published in Sibmacher's Modelbuch *of 1601.*

handed down through the generations, thereby becoming disassociated from any symbolic understanding the motifs might originally have had. It is also worth considering that pattern choices could have been made simply because a particular flower or plant was a favourite or happened to be grown in the embroiderer's garden, and so, whilst a particular flower may have had a recognised symbolic meaning, and been readily available in printed pattern books, it may not have been the primary influence in its choosing and use.

Opposite left: White work band sampler dating from the mid-seventeenth century.

Rare needle lace panel depicting a courtly couple. The detached lace on the costumes and tent flaps is relatively rarely found on white work samplers dating from the seventeenth century. This is highly complicated and would have required a high level of skill – not to mention patience – from the embroiderer.

Chapter Two

THE EIGHTEENTH CENTURY

THE early decades of the eighteenth century brought greater political, religious and economic stability to Britain than had been seen in the preceding centuries. The traditional divisions between the old landed gentry and the emerging wealthy mercantile classes based on age-old privilege and royal favour were breaking down, and society was seeing the formation of a new upper-class structure.

No longer plagued by wars and rebellions, a stronger parliamentary system of government enabled the movement towards new political reforms and growing religious tolerance. The encouragement of new trade links and emergence of new industrial and agricultural practices paved the way for a growth in a newly emerging middle class. There were the gradual signs of an increased social cohesion amongst the upper echelons of society, and a growing social and moral awareness amongst the moneyed classes towards those less fortunate members of society. Education came to be regarded as increasingly important. Needlework had always played an important role in the education of females but it had relied heavily on the traditions of the past, hence the repeated rows of different patterns and the spot motifs found on seventeenth-century samplers.

As new printed textiles became ever more available and affordable, the need to embroider domestic and household furnishings lessened. Amongst the wealthy classes the working of samplers was becoming less about recording patterns and stitches and more about the moral well-being of the young embroiderer and the social accomplishments that were expected for success in future life. Changes in the attitudes of the wealthy classes to the poor led to a growth in the founding of institutions specifically aimed at the education of their children, in an environment that would both nurture their moral well-being and provide for their future employment in the homes of the growing middle classes.

These changing attitudes to education were reflected by the samplers produced by the children of the eighteenth century, both rich and poor. Not only were samplers teaching needle skills and morality but by the end of the century were part of a broader educational curriculum. Geography, history, grammar, mathematics, and even the sciences are subjects that appear on samplers. During the eighteenth century the vast majority of samplers include some form of inscription, sometimes recording events both historical and personal. In no other century did changes to the form and content of samplers develop so rapidly.

Many early eighteenth-century samplers demonstrate the beginnings of a transition from the earlier long narrow band samplers of the seventeenth century to the squarer bordered samplers of the late eighteenth and nineteenth century.

Opposite: Mary Dean's sampler of 1729 is worked with a stag and a leopard surrounded with brightly coloured flowers and swaying trees. The inclusion of crowns is common on samplers worked during the eighteenth century.

The development or change in the shape and form of samplers did not happen suddenly, and many band samplers are found bearing eighteenth-century dates. The sampler by Abygal Muns dated 1723 is worked with many bands that would be equally at home on a sampler worked in the seventeenth century. The inclusion of several lines of inscription is, however, a feature seen with increasing frequency during the eighteenth century and marks a departure from the majority of seventeenth-century samplers, where lines of verse are less frequently included in the content of samplers. The verse at the bottom of Abygal's sampler is one that is popular on eighteenth-century samplers.

Eighteenth-century sampler worked by Abygal Muns in 1723. The bands of border patterns and the inclusion of the 'boxer' figures are reminiscent of the work of the seventeenth century.

Abygal Muns Is My Na
Me And England Is My
Nation And Aldersgate
Street Is My Dwelling
Place And Christ Is My Salvation

Marcus Huish laments in his history *Samplers and Tapestry Embroideries* (first published in 1900) 'how seldom the workers deemed it necessary to place upon them the name of the district in which they lived', but the practice of inscribing samplers with their place of origin was to become increasingly common in the eighteenth century and many variations of the verse recorded above were stitched. On a Scottish sampler the young Jean Fraser records:

Jean Fraser is my name,
Scotland is my nation,
Ardrishaig is my dwelling place,
A pleasant habitation[19]

The verse at the top of Abygal's sampler is one seen less often, but clearly indicates the importance of embroidery as a necessary skill. Abygal's father was recorded as a hackney coachman, which would have meant that Abygal's family had a comfortable upbringing.[20] Good genealogical research on samplers, where sufficient information is given for this to be possible, has enabled us to build up a picture of the backgrounds of the girls who worked different types of samplers. The assumption has been made in the past that, with the exception of plain, charity or orphanage work, samplers were the preserve of girls from wealthy backgrounds, but this sampler indicates that the desire and opportunity to educate daughters was present in all levels of society.

In Scotland the band form of sampler is often seen to have survived far later than it did in England. It is easy to see in the two samplers by Isabel and Jean Swan dated 1748 and 1752 respectively that the form of the seventeenth-century band sampler is still very much intact, even down to the inclusion of the boxer figures in the sampler worked by Jean. It is interesting to note that boxer figures are commonly found on Scottish samplers throughout the eighteenth century whilst they are relatively rare on dated eighteenth-century English examples, especially those worked later in the century.

The two lettering samplers also by Isabel and Jean Swan, and again dated 1748 and 1752 respectively, demonstrate another recognisable feature of eighteenth-

Below left: Scottish band sampler by Isabel Swan, dated 1748.

Below: Scottish band sampler by Jean Swan, dated 1752. The inclusion of boxer figures on samplers dating from later in the eighteenth century is more common on Scottish samplers than on their English counterparts.

Scottish lettering sampler by Isabel Swan, dated 1748.

Scottish lettering sampler by Jean Swan, dated 1752. The highly stylised lettering is typical of samplers worked in Scotland, as is the use of the green and red colour palette.

Far right: Continental band sampler dating from the eighteenth century. The embellished lettering is similar to that found on Scottish samplers.

century Scottish samplers and that is the limited use of colour; red and green or dark blue are the most popular colour combinations. The embellishment on the letters of the two alphabets at the bottom are another very recognisably Scottish feature, also common to many continental samplers of the period.

As the eighteenth century progressed, samplers tended to become shorter in length and started to include more lines of verse, usually of a moralistic nature. The sampler by Margaret Hopkins, dated May 1727, is typical in having several different verses alongside rows of alphabets and numerals worked in a variety of stitches. During the eighteenth century an embroidered border framing the sampler

Finely wrought eighteenth-century sampler by Frances Owen, dated 1733. Moralistic verses are common to many samplers of this period.

Margaret Hopkins's sampler worked in 1727. The inclusion of numerals and an alphabet would indicate that this sampler was produced in the classroom.

increasingly becomes a well-used device. The use of a border indicates that samplers were being worked with the intention of being framed upon completion, displayed proudly to show off a daughter's accomplishment. Martha Litchfield's sampler demonstrates the changes occurring in sampler use and design. Still of band form, the sampler is framed by a decorative floral border and incorporates a verse indicating not only how proud the young Martha was of her accomplishment, but also revealing how industry was regarded as a virtue:

Martha Litchfield is my Name, and with my Needle I Wrought the Same,
And when you View this Work of mine, Mark how Well I Spent my time
Though my Age is Small Ten Years and that's all

During the early eighteenth century a form of sampler inscribed with the Ten Commandments, the Lord's Prayer or the Creed became increasingly fashionable. Dating from around 1720, these are clearly influenced by the design of the painted wooden boards or Decalogues of the period, commonly found in churches. They are sometimes decorated with winged cherubs (guardians of paradise) in the top corners, an image also found on clock spandrels and carved church gravestones of the early eighteenth century.

The sampler worked by Ann Carter in 1720 is interesting because it tells us precisely how long it took Ann to work the sampler:

October the 19th 1719 Ann Carter began this sampler April the 6th 1720 this sampler was finished.

The inscription Ann worked between the two central tablets – 'Fear God. Honour the King' – may be connected to the fact that Elizabeth I reputedly ordered the royal coat of arms to be placed in all churches over the inscribed wooden tablet boards. The boards were intended to show the essential teaching of the Christian faith and by the inclusion of royal arms the legality of the monarch as the supreme head of the Church of England. During the Commonwealth period (1649–60) many coats of arms were destroyed; of the very few earlier examples that survive, the most famous is in the church of St Mary in Preston, Suffolk.

Martha Litchfield worked an embroidered border to enclose her sampler, clearly indicating the intention to frame and display the sampler. The fact that many original frames exist that date from the eighteenth century indicates that this was common practice.

Ann Carter's sampler dated 1720 indicates precisely how long she took to work this typical example.

Above right: A highly decorative Decalogue or tablet sampler worked by Elizabeth Harryman, dating from the mid eighteenth century.

A very similar sampler to Ann Carter's sampler is in the collection of the Victoria and Albert Museum, London, worked by Eleanor Speed between 12 December and 6 May 1784. This demonstrates that many forms of sampler design remained in fashion over long periods of time and that their evolution could be a slow process, particularly in some of the remoter parts of the country.

The inclusion of Moses and Aaron on tablet samplers is not uncommon during the eighteenth century. The two illustrated examples by Elizabeth Harryman and Martha C. show two very different techniques. Martha's sampler is worked entirely in tent stitch, which leaves none of the ground material showing. The tassels and the fringing decorating the heavily draped curtain have been enhanced by the use of metallic threads, also used to highlight the border around the central tablets and parts of Aaron's costume. Elizabeth's sampler is worked in bright floss silks, employing a variety of stitches to enhance its decorative appeal. The bottom portion of Elizabeth's sampler incorporates various animals: a stag, squirrel, sheep, rabbit, cow, and dog placed in a verdant grassy setting.

During the eighteenth century the education of the daughters of the middle classes tended to be carried out either in the home under the instruction of a private tutor, or at one of the increasingly numerous female academies or small dame schools. The sampler worked by Sarah Chamberlain in 1751 was worked in just such an establishment run by Sarah Dawber. Genealogical research reveals that Sarah Chamberlain was baptised in St Stephen's Church, Norwich, on 22 October 1741, making her ten years old when she worked her sampler. Sarah Dawber, also from Norwich (baptised at St Giles's Church in 1703), never married but set up a small school in the town in order to earn a living. Becoming a schoolteacher was seen as a respectable profession for women, and there are numerous instances of either single or widowed ladies setting up their own small schools to provide for themselves and any children they might have.

Local newspaper adverts and trade cards dating from the eighteenth century exist showing that the subjects taught in these schools tended to be fairly constant: English, French, geography, arithmetic, writing, music, drawing, dancing, and needlework. The rare musical sampler, as well as the two samplers by Elizabeth Oxley (1754) and by Ann Lock (1761), are likely to have been worked at such a

Tablet sampler worked by Martha C. in London in the 1730s.

Sampler worked by Sarah Chamberlain under the instruction of Sarah Dawber in 1751.

school. We know they were worked under the instruction of the same teacher, but the existence of two further examples dated around the same time as these two samplers, both held in private collections, suggest that Mary Hewart ran her own school rather than working as a private governess.[21]

These two samplers, although not identical, have many design elements in common. The side borders are worked with the same meandering flower heads although they are not necessarily worked in the exact same colours or combination. The central box does not contain the same verse but the order in which the various elements are placed, such as the alphabet and rows of numerals, is the same. The two scenes appearing at the centre top of the samplers are different (the Angel appearing to the shepherds on Elizabeth's sampler and the Angel appearing to Mary on the sampler by Ann), but both are taken from the New Testament. The extent to which the samplers were the design of the teacher or the pupil is difficult to ascertain. It is certainly true that it is often possible to recognise the samplers worked under the tuition of a particular schoolteacher.

It is not just the elements of the design that are common to both samplers; it is also the choice of stitches and coloured silks chosen to complete the work. The same choice of stitch is made for the same elements of the two samplers, so the stems of the floral chains are both worked in chain stitch whilst the petals of the flower heads are worked in long and short stitch. It seems probable that Mary Hewart had her repertoire of favoured biblical stories from which to draw, and a format for the teaching of samplers. The girls may or may not have had a say in the individual choices of elements that were to make up their finished sampler.

Engraving of the trade card of Mrs Masquerier's Boarding School, Kensington.

Although we do not know the precise source of the designs for either of these samplers or indeed many other samplers, it would seem highly likely that many samplers took designs from pattern books and printed sources. The Angel appearing to the Virgin Mary on the sampler by Ann Lock bears a striking resemblance to the angels that often appear on seventeenth-century embroidered pictures and cushion covers. The treatment of the oak trees on both samplers with their oversized acorns cannot help but remind us of the trees found on seventeenth-century tent stitch work. A question to which we will perhaps never know the answer is: who drew out the design of the sampler? Did the teacher draw the design or was the drawing part of the lesson? Certainly we know drawing lessons were part of the curriculum at many schools at this period.

The sampler worked by Elizabeth Coker in 1728 demonstrates that needlework was combined with the teaching of other subjects, in this case French. The Lord's Prayer worked in French is combined with rows of alphabets and a decorative band of solid cross stitch. In this sampler Elizabeth has included a band that incorporates fifteen crowns and coronets; these devices were used to denote titles such as baron, viscount and duke, and would have been incorporated on the household linen of families who attained these high ranks. Crowns and coronets are often incorporated onto samplers

Above: Rare musical sampler worked with the notes of a cotillion. The cotillion was a dance introduced from France to London in around 1766. It became very popular in late eighteenth-century society.

A sampler worked by Elizabeth Oxley under the instruction of Mrs Hewart in 1754. The practice of recording the embroiderer's date of birth is not seen very frequently. Dates and ages are often found to have been unpicked on surviving samplers.

47

Eighteenth-century sampler worked by Ann Lock under the instruction of Mrs Hewart. This sampler was worked seven years after Elizabeth Oxley's sampler. A third, almost identical sampler, by Mary Portus, is also known to have been worked under the instruction of the same Mary Hewart.

worked by girls who would be likely to go into service, but the fact that Elizabeth is receiving instruction in French suggests that she was being educated at a private school and therefore less likely to seek a position in service. It would seem more likely that for Elizabeth she chose to include the crowns and coronets simply for their decorative appeal. An Elizabeth Coker has been identified as being born in Fareham (Hampshire) in 1716, which would make her a possible candidate for the working of this sampler. (The dates of no other eligible Elizabeth Coker are recorded.) This would provide a possible explanation for the inclusion of the Lord's Prayer in French, since by the eighteenth century Fareham had had a long association with France both through trade and as a town with a strong naval and boat-building tradition.

The tablet sampler worked in 1734 by Anne Marbeuf also includes the Lord's Prayer and the Creed in French. Anne came from a French Huguenot family and it may well be that the family still spoke French in the home, and wanted their children to learn and maintain the French language. It is not indicated on the sampler whether the sampler was worked within the household or at a school, but

Elizabeth Coker's sampler has the Lord's Prayer worked in French.

in Westminster at the time of the working of the sampler there would be a choice of schools teaching the French language. London had a large Huguenot population during the eighteenth century. It is worth noting that despite being worked in French by a Huguenot girl, the form of the sampler is not one that would be found on the Continent. Unlike English samplers, those worked on the Continent rarely contain inscriptions apart from alphabets, names, initials or dates.

Later in the century the fashion for pastoral subjects, popularised in paintings of the period, is seen on samplers. It is generally assumed that the use of these more decorative subjects often denotes the work of the daughters of the wealthy classes. Increasingly comfortable upholstered seat furniture was finding its way into these households and much of the canvas-worked upholstery, whether worked within the house or professionally worked and bought in, included pastoral subjects. The sampler worked by Mary Susannah Lambeth in 1780 combines a pastoral scene with the tablet form discussed earlier.

This extraordinarily accomplished sampler, flawlessly embroidered with brightly coloured silks on a cream wool ground is at the pinnacle of English sampler-making during the eighteenth century. The sampler is divided into three parts, a not uncommon arrangement on samplers of the eighteenth century. The upper section is of a traditional form with bands of alphabets, numerals, border designs and an inscription. The middle section consists of two tablets inscribed with a long religious text, headed with the name of Mary Susannah's governess. The tablets are divided with a basket of mixed flowers worked in brightly coloured silks, and above the tablets is rich red drapery with swags and tassels, held up by two angels. The bottom section, predominantly worked in minute tent stitch, provides the major decorative

Ann Marbeuf's sampler worked in London in French. Ann came from a Huguenot family, so it is possible that French was spoken within the home.

element of the sampler. The scene shows gentlefolk in an idealised country setting following country pursuits: the two ladies are dressed as shepherdesses whilst the gentleman is fishing. This scene represents the height of late eighteenth-century fashionable taste, and was a popular subject on all manner of interior decoration including furniture, porcelain, textiles and wallpaper.

It is hard to conceive that this outstanding eighteenth-century sampler was worked by Mary Susannah Lambeth when she was just ten years old.

It is possible to see the original pencil drawn outline in the branches of the oak tree on this anonymous sampler. The proportions of the figures are somewhat distorted, giving the sampler a charming quality.

Canvas work intended for upholstery or simply as a picture was a very popular pastime during the late eighteenth century. Idealised country scenes were amongst the most popular subjects and the shepherdess sitting surrounded by her sheep and occasional cattle was perhaps the most popular image of all. Many of the patterns for canvas work were imported from France, as was much of the finished embroidered upholstery fabric used by the fashionable furniture makers of the time. The choice of expensive floss silk threads, the fashionable subject and the employment of a governess to teach the young Mary Susannah are all clues to her social class and likely economic status.

The anonymous sampler illustrated on this page, whilst very different from that worked by Mary Susannah Lambeth, illustrates the popularity of the couple in an idealised country setting dressed as shepherd and shepherdess. The top portion of the sampler is worked with alphabets, border patterns, crowns and coronets, and a verse taken from Proverbs, and is in all respects very typical of the samplers of the eighteenth century. The sampler relies entirely on the bottom panel for its decorative effect. It is just possible to make out the drawn outline of the figures and the animals in this sampler. That this sampler was drawn out by the anonymous embroiderer and not her teacher seems probable when you examine the shepherdess's right arm, which has a reach longer than her body.

Freely worked samplers, in which at least parts of the design do not entirely rely on counted thread work, became popular during the eighteenth century. In the unfinished sampler worked by Elizabeth Pleasance in 1749, it is possible to see the drawn design worked on to the ground prior to being embroidered. Worked with a broad floral border, this sampler is in contrast to the counted thread work that was to become so popular in the nineteenth century. Possibly because the sampler was never finished and therefore not framed it has retained its original colour. It is rare to find completed samplers that still retain their entire original colour.

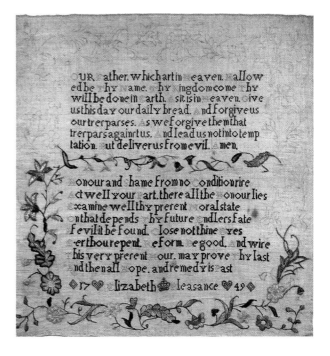

Darning samplers are another distinct form of sampler dating from the eighteenth century. Darning samplers originated in northern Europe in the early eighteenth century and spread to England and North America later on in the eighteenth century. The original purpose was to teach the mending of textiles of different fabrics and weaves. Textiles were considered valuable commodities and as such were often passed down from one generation to another through families, thus their repair was a necessity to prolong the useful life of such articles.

Darning aims by the insertion of additional threads into the warp and weft of the cloth to repair holes and tears by copying the original fabric weave, the most common weaves being tabby, web, damask and twill. The darning sampler was an exercise in perfecting the technique required for such repair work. Many darning samplers consist of a series of crosses arranged on the fabric and worked in contrasting coloured silks in a series of different weaves. In some cases an actual hole was cut into the fabric, which then had to be darned.

The continental sampler illustrated on page 54 is worked with shades of deep red, green and blue, making it easy to see the darning stitches. This contrasts starkly with the sampler worked by Mary Bailey in 1799, probably under Quaker instruction but almost certainly in an institutional environment rather than in the home. Mary has included at the centre of two of her darns some decorative drawn work stitches. The skill to darn white linens and the fine white muslin used in baby clothes as well as female undergarments would have been a necessity for girls likely to go into service. Many white work darning samplers were worked in charity schools and orphanages, and it seems likely that economy may be one reason why this necessary skill was learnt by working white thread on a white ground.

The sampler by Mary Hornsby, and the example initialled 'ME' and dated 1806, are in marked contrast to both the white work and the continental samplers. They are far more decorative in their design and show a wider use of different techniques. The sampler by Mary, with its central vase of flowers, was not worked simply to

Above left: White darning sampler by Mary Bailey, possibly worked under the tuition of a teacher at a Quaker school.

Above: This unfinished sampler by Elizabeth Pleasance allows us to see clearly the hand drawn design which was in part embroidered over. Relatively few unfinished samplers survive, encouraging the theory that many were thrown out over the following years. Perhaps if a child had died suddenly a parent would not want to keep the sampler in the home. Embroidered on fine muslin, the text on samplers worked at charity schools is often worked in red thread, the most economical to purchase.

Continental darning sampler. This utilitarian sampler is typical of those worked in northern Europe in the eighteenth and nineteenth centuries.

show her darning skills, but was worked as a decorative piece in its own right. Although it still incorporates four darning crosses in each corner, it is likely to have been worked at one of the female academies set up to educate the children of the middle classes.

As is true in many areas of study, it is easy to make generalisations, and whilst it is true that very often charity schools teaching needlework for practical and necessary purposes worked relatively plain darning samplers, often using a limited colour palette, the sampler worked by Esther Walker in 1841 proves that not all work undertaken at such institutions was plain. Embroidered onto a fine muslin using coloured silks, this darning sampler bears testament to the standard of teaching and embroidery skills which could be achieved by girls of humble origin. Although later in date than the previous examples, the inclusion of moral text, whilst commonplace on orphanage and charity work, is unusual in its combination with darning techniques.

What is generally regarded as the first printed geography text appeared in England in 1625: *Geography delineated forth in two bookes*, published by Nathaniel Carpenter. During the course of the seventeenth century other geography texts followed;

A rare darning sampler worked at Mr Raine's Asylum in 1841.

Below left: English darning sampler worked in 1801. The border of leaves worked in different darning stitches is unusual.

Below: A fine and highly decorative darning sampler by Mary Hornsby, dated 1798. The decorative darning samplers are thought to have frequently been worked at small, privately run dame schools.

Advertisement for Miss Lane's school at Truro Vean, Truro, Cornwall. It is interesting to note the range of subjects offered, as well as the fees charged, by these private girls' schools during the eighteenth and nineteenth centuries.

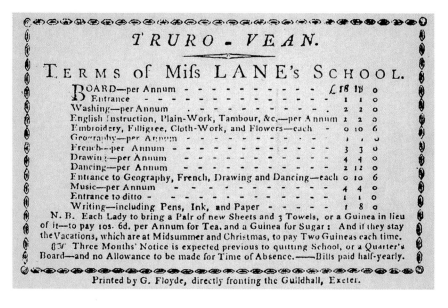

Map sampler worked at a school in Tottenham by Margaret Jermyn in 1787.

This map sampler by Hannah Bailey is probably worked at the same school as the sampler by Margaret Jermyn two years earlier.

however, it was not until the eighteenth century that geographies and gazetteers appeared in any great numbers. In 1693 Patrick Gordon had published a small illustrated geography book entitled *Geography Anatomised or The Geographical Grammar*. By 1754 nineteen editions of this work had appeared, sporadically updated with new engravings of maps. By 1800 over four hundred different geographies that included maps had been published.[22]

It is against this background that we see from the 1770s onwards the emerging fashion for the working of map samplers in schools. Map samplers were worked not only as exercises in stitching but also as an acceptable means of teaching geography to young ladies. Contemporary adverts for ladies' boarding schools list geography amongst the subjects taught. Firms such as Laurie & Whittle, founded in 1794, produced printed maps specifically for young ladies to copy in needlework.

Embroidered maps were produced in a number of ways. In some cases a teacher or pupil would trace a map on to a ground cloth from a printed paper source, often an existing engraving, perhaps reusing the original printed paper map many

This fine map of Scotland worked on a silk satin ground was produced especially for needleworkers. It was first published by Laurie & Whittle in 1797.

times. Evidence of this practice is revealed by a number of embroidered maps worked at the same Tottenham school, which although not identical are quite clearly worked from the same print source, in this case *An accurate Map of England and Wales laid down from the best authorities* by Emmanuel Bowen, first published in 1754. The cartouche appearing in the top right hand corner of both maps illustrating a monument is taken from a cartouche used by Bowen in which the titles of his maps appear in their printed versions. Bowen produced a series of maps in conjunction with Thomas Kitchin, who, as well as being an author, engraver and publisher himself, had a shop selling artists' materials in Holborn Hill, London. It would be from just such an emporium that the ladies who ran girls' schools would have purchased those items necessary for their lessons.

On other occasions maps printed on to a silk ground were purchased, ready to be embroidered directly onto. *A New Map of Scotland for Ladies Needlework*, published by Laurie & Whittle of No. 53 Fleet Street in January 1797, is one such example. Priced at 7s 6d this would have been an expensive purchase, almost certainly available only to the daughters of wealthy parents who could pay for the private education offered by

An exceptionally fine map of the world worked at E. Price's school by Mary Ann Reynolds in Worcester in 1789. These double hemisphere maps were worked at schools in both Britain and America.

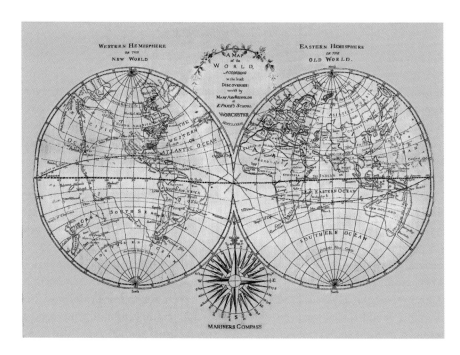

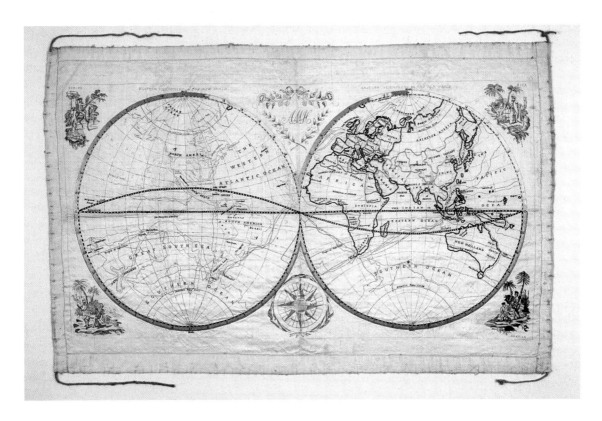

the growing number of ladies' boarding schools. Interestingly, this map was also available as a thin paper template, which could then be laid over a fabric ground and then stitched through. Paper versions of this map are held in the collections of the National Library of Scotland and the Scottish Geographical Society. Perhaps not entirely coincidentally, Laurie & Whittle's premises were in Fleet Street, not far from those of Emmanuel Bowen.

The most common subject found on surviving map samplers is undoubtedly England with part of Scotland, Ireland, the English Channel and a small part of northern France. Maps of Europe also exist in reasonably large numbers. Maps of individual foreign countries, counties of England, and even individual farms exist but are far rarer.

Amongst the most complicated and skilful maps worked are double hemisphere world maps, produced both in America and England during the late eighteenth century. These maps not only show the countries of the world as they were then known but often reflected the growing interest and awareness of the growth in trade routes and modern exploration. 'A Map of the World According to the latest Discoveries work'd by Mary Ann Reynolds at E Prices school, Worcester' in 1789 includes the mariner's compass together with various explorations, including the routes of Cook's voyages in 1770 and 1775, his track north and return south.

The rare unfinished world map initialled 'MAH', complete with its linen band edging and fastening strings at each corner, shows where it would have been attached to a frame. Because of its unfinished state it can quite clearly be seen that

This unfinished double hemisphere sampler provides us with a rare opportunity for study. Clearly hand drawn, the sampler is complete with its original fastening strings.

This rare globe sampler is believed to have been worked at Westtown School in America. No globe samplers are known with a British or continental origin.

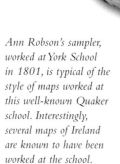

Ann Robson's sampler, worked at York School in 1801, is typical of the style of maps worked at this well-known Quaker school. Interestingly, several maps of Ireland are known to have been worked at the school.

this map has been drawn or traced by hand onto the ground fabric. The four continents carefully drawn in each corner, and in the case of America partially worked in black silk, are clearly copied from or strongly influenced by the engravings found on printed maps of the period.

When considering the precision needed to complete these complicated and often technically challenging pieces, it is easy to see why they would have needed to be fixed to a frame, and why it is thought that in many cases these were the finale to a girl's education, to be framed and displayed as a proud accomplishment.

Embroidered maps worked on to a flat ground were worked in both Europe and America in many schools but perhaps amongst the rarest form of sampler known are the terrestrial and celestial globe samplers worked at Westtown School in America. The production of globe samplers was a highly complicated exercise. First a number of pieces of shaped linen (usually eight) had to be cut, stitched, and stuffed to form an even sphere. This was then covered with an equal number of similarly shaped sections of silk, which had been marked with either the geographical or astronomical details to be shown on the finished globe. These segments of silk were then stitched onto the linen ground and embroidered.

The Quaker school at Westtown is known to have produced globe samplers, but it is interesting to note that, despite the fact that Westtown was set up to be run on the same lines as Ackworth School in England, no globe samplers are known to have been worked at Ackworth. In fact, despite many common similarities and features shared by the needlework samplers of America and England, no English school is known to have produced globe samplers. One possible theory as to why globes were worked only in America is that it was not until 1810 that globes were manufactured in America by James Wilson. Until this date the necessity to import globes for teaching geography would have been prohibitively expensive. In England the Quaker school at York is also known to have produced a relatively large number of maps, as is Mountmellick School in Ireland.

The working of embroidered maps continued into the nineteenth century but perhaps due to changing methods of teaching in general and geography in particular, and the increased availability of printed atlases, the practice had with very few exceptions died out by the middle of the nineteenth century.

Towards the end of the eighteenth century the expansion of the subjects taught to girls is reflected

A history of England from William the Conqueror to the present time. This unusual history sampler stands as testament to the broad curriculum taught to girls in the late eighteenth century.

in the samplers which survive from that date. The history of England, which although undated was almost certainly worked in the late eighteenth century, clearly indicates that geography was not the only subject for which samplers provided a method of teaching. A second history sampler (not illustrated) remains unfinished and could perhaps indicate the death of the young scholar, or perhaps a very sudden change in the fortunes of the family. The changes that occur in the development of samplers towards the end of the eighteenth century are not simply confined to the variety of subjects included on samplers. Towards the end of the eighteenth century the ground fabric on which samplers were worked also becomes more varied, and fine cottons such as muslin, tiffany and gauze become more popular. Perhaps this is influenced by the use of lightweight fabrics in the making of the most fashionable dresses of the period. Indeed the two histories are worked on an exceptionally fine linen.

HARVEST

Fountain of mercy! God of love!
How rich thy bounties are,
The rolling seasons as they move,
Proclaim thy constant care.

When in the bosom of the earth
The sower hid his grain,
Thy goodness marked its secret birth,
And sent the early rain.

The springs sweet influence was thine,
The plants in beauty grew,
Thou gav'st refulgent suns to shine,
And mild refreshing dew.

These various mercies from above
Matured the swelling grain;
A kindly harvest crowns thy love,
And plenty fills the plain.

Maria Lamb. Croydon School 1841.

Chapter Three

QUAKER SAMPLERS

Until very recently the samplers produced at the many and varied Quaker schools across both Britain and America were little understood. It is only relatively recently that serious study has enabled us to understand and appreciate this distinctive group of samplers.

Founded in England in the early 1650s by George Fox (1624–91), the early Quaker movement began as a breakaway movement from English Puritanism. The middle years of the seventeenth century were a time of great political turmoil, when King Charles I was struggling to retain his right to 'divine rule' against the growing strength of the fledgling Parliamentary movement. During the ensuing first Civil War (1642–9) his influence over the established church had weakened and a number of free-thinking groups and alternative religious sects were established. On his accession to power Oliver Cromwell had found it necessary to take charge of the Church of England, making dissenting religions illegal, and he introduced fines and imprisonment for non-attendance and non-payment of tithes.

Against this background the young George Fox, who came from strongly Puritan roots, became increasingly disillusioned with the established church and its clergy. In contrast with the establishment, Fox believed that God could speak to men and women directly without the need for either church or priest. He believed that both men and women had equal rights to minister, and his stand against swearing oaths or paying tithes, most of which went to the established church or absentee landlords, brought him into conflict with the establishment. From his first public speech in 1647 until his first vision in 1651 George Fox spent his time travelling the country preaching, and was imprisoned in Derby jail for preaching his beliefs. By 1652 he had 'convinced' over 1,000 followers, including Margaret Fell, whose home, Swarthmore Hall, was to become the unofficial centre of the Quaker ministry. Much of the work undertaken here involved distributing funds to the growing group of missionaries, receiving and forwarding communications between the group's members, holding meetings and providing a place of refuge for its members.

During the early seventeenth century the persecution of these early Quakers led to a separation from the establishment, and, whilst not without their disputes, the society's belief in social justice, the rights of women, and opportunity for all led to the formation of close bonds between groups of Quakers who were geographically separated from each other. By the standards of the seventeenth century many Quakers travelled widely, as far afield as America, Newfoundland, the West Indies, as well as continental Europe. In 1681 the foundation of Pennsylvania by the Quaker William Penn had cemented the Quaker family as an international movement, and by 1689 the Act of Toleration enabled them to assemble freely, sharing their values and ideas.

Opposite: Maria Lamb's extract sampler worked at Croydon School in 1841 is typical of the many extract samplers worked under Quaker instruction, and may be compared to those worked at Ackworth.

From the very earliest years Quakers took a keen interest in the education of their children, both male and female. In 1668 George Fox himself founded two schools, one at Waltham Abbey and a second girls' school at Shacklewell, 'set up to instruct young lasses and maidens in what so ever things were civil and useful in the creation'.[23] At a time when female education generally received little support the Quakers proved to be uncommonly enlightened.

Despite the efforts and beliefs of the early Quakers, progress in establishing a strong network of schools was difficult, particularly during the early years of the eighteenth century. Quakers, in common with other nonconformists, were barred from university entrance and so relatively few of them entered the professions. Instead, the more ambitious Quakers channelled their efforts into business. The success and growing prosperity of this group of Quakers led to a schism between them and the devout 'plain' Quakers who lived a simple, more isolated and less worldly existence. For both groups education was an important consideration, and whilst the prosperous urban businessmen could afford to send their children to school, the poor, particularly those living in rural areas, had little access to education. Many of the charity schools at this time were open only to members of the Church of England.

In 1758 the committee of the London Yearly Meeting commissioned a report into the education of members of the Society of Friends. In 1759 the report found that there were twenty-one small boarding schools including the Clerkenwell Workhouse School (founded in 1702 by John Bellars) and numerous small day schools providing a simple education. It was felt by the committee that the educational provision was inadequate and a second 'special committee of meetings for sufferings' was set up to consider the existing state of education within the Society of Friends. In 1760 the committee reported that the number of schools was

This landscape-shaped medallion sampler is worked on a coarse linen ground with a limited palette of coloured silk threads. The three confronting pairs of birds are similar although not identical to those worked on the medallion sampler initialled 'SB' and dated 1776.

insufficient, being able to educate only 630 Quaker children, and that there were not enough skilled teachers, and Quaker schools produced too few 'scholars of repute'. It was noted that due to the low standards being achieved in Quaker schools a number of members were sending their children to schools unconnected with the Society of Friends.

Amongst the committee was Dr John Fothergill, an eminent London physician who had been born in Yorkshire in 1712 and educated at Sedbergh before being apprenticed to a Quaker apothecary at the age of sixteen. Dr Fothergill was physician to the Clerkenwell Workhouse. His father had travelled widely in America, an interest he had passed on to his son, who took a keen interest in American affairs and became a friend of Benjamin Franklin.

In 1777 the London Yearly Meeting minuted that they were to encourage the founding of a boarding school for the children of parents who were not in affluence. In 1778 Dr Fothergill whilst travelling in Yorkshire became aware that the buildings of the Foundling Hospital at Ackworth were for sale. Not one to delay, and with the agreement of the Yearly Meeting, Dr Fothergill (who personally guaranteed the £7,000 purchase price) founded Ackworth School, taking possession of the buildings on Lady Day 1778 and taking in its first scholars on 18 October 1779.

Right from its inception Ackworth was experimental in the education it offered, mixing both manual work with academic learning. To quote Dr Fothergill, 'Learning and labour properly intermixed greatly assist the ends of both.' Whilst the boys were expected to wait at table and help in the bakery, farm and dairy, the girls shared the domestic duties of the school, mending linen, waiting on the housekeepers' table and assisting with the laundry and mantua making.

Sarah Grubb records:

> The girls are provided with work by the institution; and, for their improvement, finer needlework than the family can furnish them with, is taken in for hire; when that falls short, childbed linen is sometimes made to sell in which superfluous work is guarded against.[24]

It is important to consider that, at a time when all clothing and household linen was hand worked, demonstrating needle skills was essential for girls who were likely to

Numerous confronting pairs and single birds appear on this medallion sampler which predates the founding of Ackworth School. This sampler, worked onto a fine linen background, has one later-worked medallion in the top left corner; the rest would all appear to have been worked in 1776.

be apprenticed or go into service. So in a school that was initially set up for the children of families who were 'not in affluence' it is not surprising that needlework should form an important part of the curriculum. That the daughters of the poor should be taught to write was more unusual.

The samplers of Ackworth are important because prior to its foundation it is hard to distinguish the vast majority of Quaker samplers from those worked by non-Quakers. For the daughters of those Quakers who were in a position to educate them, it seems their samplers reflected the conventions prevalent at the time of their working. This could well be the result of the many affluent Quaker families who sent their daughters to schools not run by Quakers. The development of the distinctive style of samplers produced at Ackworth spread not only to other Quaker schools elsewhere in Britain but also to those founded in America.

There are two basic styles of sampler that have become associated with Ackworth and the Quaker schools which followed its foundation. Medallion samplers were long believed to have been developed at Ackworth and worked either at the same time or very shortly afterwards at Esther Tuke's school in Trinity Lane, York. From dated examples it was believed that this style of sampler developed around 1789–90. That the two schools should share common designs was not surprising, since Esther's two daughters both attended Ackworth and Esther herself was a visitor at Ackworth (the term 'visitor' would have much the same meaning as a modern-day school governor). The sampler initialled 'MS' (Mary Storr) and dated 1791 is an early example of an Ackworth medallion sampler. However, recently two medallion samplers predating the foundation of Ackworth have come to light. The sampler initialled 'SB' and dated 1776 is amongst the earliest dated medallion samplers to have been discovered.

The origin of the medallions is something of a mystery. It had been suggested that the appearance of medallions at both Ackworth and Esther Tuke's school at York at around the same time could perhaps be the result of the teaching of an individual who worked at both schools, the 30-mile distance between them making this entirely possible. The other possibility is that they were taken from a pattern book, although as yet no such pattern book has been found.[25]

This medallion sampler worked by Ann Davis at Ackworth in 1807 is believed to be dedicated to the same Martha Deane who in 1811 worked a sampler dedicated to Ann Davis. Notice the letters of the alphabet placed in between the medallions (this feature is not found on Martha's sampler).

The medallion samplers worked at Ackworth have several variations. A large number of the surviving examples are worked on an open weave linen in a dark green or brown thread. The sampler worked by Ann Davis is typical of this type of medallion sampler. It is interesting to note that, as shown in this example, Ackworth samplers often contain sets of initials. In this sampler there is the dedication 'AD to MD 1807'. The 'AD' is almost certainly the Ann Davis who worked the sampler, whilst the 'MD' probably refers to Martha Deane (a scholar 1805–11), who was in Ann's year group. It is believed that the samplers were often dedicated to fellow classmates and the working of a similar medallion sampler with the initials 'MD to AD' and the dedication 'A TOKEN OF LOVE' is probably not simply coincidental.

This medallion sampler, almost certainly worked by Martha Deane at Ackworth, is dedicated to 'AD', believed to be Ann Davis. The practice of dedicating samplers to fellow scholars is not uncommon at Quaker schools.

The children who attended Ackworth came from all over the country and indeed from as far away as Australia, Russia and America.[26] From the opening of the school the girls and boys were strictly segregated, often meaning that siblings were kept apart. It was not until sixty-eight years after the founding of the school in 1847 that annual holidays were introduced. Prior to this date, once a child entered the school they could remain there for several years, rarely stepping into the outside world. Thus it is not surprising that the children formed close relationships with fellow pupils and dedicated their samplers to each other.

In the advertisement for Esther Tuke's proposed boarding school for girls she states:

> The Education of Friends Children in general, especially Girls, consistent with the Principles we profess, having been the subject of solid consideration with divers Friends, who have beheld with satisfaction the advantages derived from ACKWORTH SCHOOL, and are desirous that a similar opportunity of a guarded Education may be extended to such Girls, who, by reason of their Age, or on account of the circumstances of their Parents or Friends, are not sent thither.[27]

This advert serves to remind us of just how highly regarded the education offered by Ackworth was amongst the Quaker population at the end of the eighteenth century, but it also makes it plain that this private school was not for the daughters of the poor.

The sampler worked by Hannah Wallis and dated 1802 is a fine example of a group of medallion samplers worked in bright silk on fine linen grounds. These samplers illustrate the anomaly between the values considered important by a Quaker institution dedicated to the teaching of its children and the decorative quality of the work it produced. The coloured medallions were produced over a

Worked in brightly coloured silk thread on a fine linen ground, this sampler provides a stark contrast to the medallions worked in muted colours on coarser grounds.

'A Prayer for Wisdom', worked by Ann Hancock in 1789, is typical of the early Ackworth extracts. Later in the nineteenth century the variety of verses worked on the extracts becomes less varied.

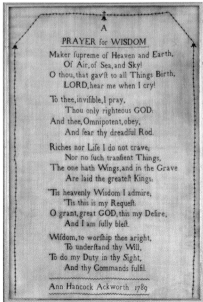

comparatively short period of time from about 1790 until about 1820. The Ackworth medallion samplers display a wide variety of complexity: those worked on coarse linen with large stitches could indicate that the girl had simply not achieved the same level of proficiency as that of the girl who worked a fine polychrome medallion sampler. However, the existence of two samplers, one a course monochrome medallion, the other a finer polychrome medallion, worked by the same girl, Ann Trump, in the same year 1797 could indicate that the two types of sampler were worked for different purposes. It is possible that the larger scale samplers could have been worked as examples to be copied, thereby teaching the principle of counting threads. It is equally possible that they were simply practice pieces before the girls worked their finer samplers using more expensive silks. By the early nineteenth century the girls attending Ackworth were coming from a wider variety of backgrounds; not all were the daughters of impoverished families, indeed a number of relatively prosperous families were sending their children to Ackworth.

Certainly we know that whilst there were no school holidays, some children received visits from parents or other relations, and that the children on occasion received packages and gifts. It is not inconceivable that coloured silks were included in these packages, for the girls to work gifts or even make items to sell.

The foundation of Ackworth can be seen to have directly influenced the foundation of other Quaker schools, whether open to the children of those who were in poverty or otherwise. The styles of samplers worked at the different Quaker schools can be seen to be very similar. The sampler worked by Maria Lamb at Croydon School can be compared to the extract samplers worked at Ackworth.

The extract samplers worked not just at Ackworth but at many of the Quaker schools across the country form a visually recognisable group. The inclusion of morally uplifting verse is common to many samplers of the eighteenth and nineteenth centuries, but it is the simplicity of the Quaker extract samplers which marks them out from samplers worked by the children of non-Quaker families. Quaker extract samplers are almost without exception worked in monochrome thread, usually black, but occasionally red or dark blue. The extract samplers worked during the eighteenth century display a little more variety of verse, whereas those worked in the nineteenth century tend to display less variety, 'Solitude', 'Virtue' and 'Resignation' being amongst the most popular.[28]

The sampler worked by Mary Hartas at York School in 1791 contains many of the same conventions as appear on the mixed marking and extract samplers produced at Ackworth during the same period, and indeed the name Hartas appears in the list of scholars attending Ackworth during the nineteenth century, providing yet more evidence of the family ties linking the wider Quaker community and the schools that served it.[29] Samplers are known to have been worked by sisters from the Strode family at Quaker schools as far apart as Ackworth in Yorkshire and Sidcot in Somerset. Of other Quaker schools producing samplers that share very similar characteristics perhaps one of the best known is Milverton, and again it is possible to find family connections linking its scholars to other Quaker schools.

In 1878 the Quakers inaugurated the Friends' Schools Industrial Exhibition to

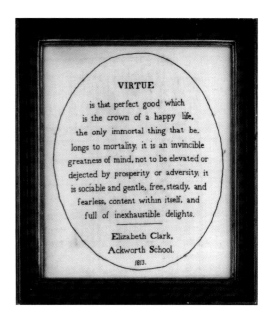

Of the many Quaker extracts worked at Ackworth the majority are worked in an oval embroidered frame. 'Virtue', 'Solitude', 'Religion', and 'Blessed' are amongst the most commonly found extracts.

Mary Hartas's sampler worked at York School in 1791 follows many of the same conventions as oval mixed-content samplers worked at other Quaker schools. Several very similar samplers are held in the archive at Ackworth.

The sampler worked by Ann Trusted at Milverton does not include a date, although it would seem probable from surviving records that Ann worked this sampler in the last years of the eighteenth century.

The alphabet sampler worked by Jane Graham at Wigton in 1819 uses the same typical Quaker lettering common to all Quaker samplers.

encourage children attending Quaker schools to use their leisure time productively. The exhibitions were held for five years between 1878 and 1882; the first two were held at Ackworth, after which they were held at Sidcot, Penketh, and lastly at Ayton. In the first year the exhibition was open only to boys; however, in the remaining four years girls could also enter. The exhibitions comprised different categories including needlework, for which prizes of money were awarded to those whose work was judged to be the best (10 shillings for the first prize, 5 shillings for the second prize, and 2 shillings and 6 pence for the third place). The prize winners were also awarded medals – it is perhaps evidence of the importance of Ackworth that on the reverse of the medal awarded in 1880 to Alice Burton of Penketh School for her needlework we see the profile of Dr John Fothergill, founder of Ackworth School. The casting of the profile on the medal is the same as that on the centenary medals, which were awarded to every Ackworth scholar in 1879 to celebrate the foundation of the school.

Although not strictly speaking samplers, pin balls are often collected by sampler collectors and enthusiasts and it is for this reason that they have been included here. Before mass production pins were precious and expensive items treasured by their owners. Knitted pincushions were therefore popular accessories and had been made and used for many hundreds of years. Like sewing, knitting was a skill which was considered a necessity for many young women, particularly those from poorer backgrounds. Before the mechanisation of the knitting industry all stockings and socks had to be knitted by hand and so they were expensive items to purchase. The ability to knit could supplement the income of a working family, whilst allowing the woman to be at home to attend to the needs of her family.

That pin balls have come to be associated with Quaker schools and Ackworth in particular is perhaps not surprising – we know that the girls not only had to provide for the needs of the scholars themselves, but also took in work from the outside community, and knitting enabled them to earn extra income. During the eighteenth century knitting had become a more acceptable pastime for the wealthy classes, and the production of small objects such as pin balls knitted in silk became fashionable and they were often worked as gifts.

It seems from the relatively large number that survive from the eighteenth and nineteenth centuries that pin balls were worked at Quaker schools not as part of their lessons but in their leisure time, either as gifts or to

This rare medal, presented to Alice Burton of Penketh School in 1880 as a prize in a needlework competition, bears the same profile of Dr John Fothergill as the centenary medal awarded to Ackworth scholars in 1879.

sell. In 1823 Caroline Stickney, an Ackworth scholar, wrote to a friend, acknowledging her debt, 'which I hope a few pin cushions I have to sell will repay.'[30] The fact that it is not uncommon to find the name of the institution where the pin ball was worked, and that many of them include typical Quaker motifs, encourages the theory of a connection with the Quaker movement, although it may be that schools such as Ackworth were simply reflecting what was happening in other schools that took in the children of the poor during this period.

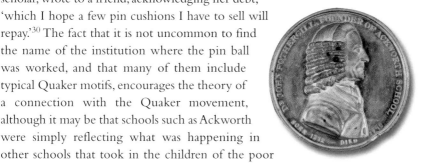

Above: This centenary medal was presented to an Ackworth scholar to mark the first hundred years of the school's founding. The medals were the gift of several prominent Quaker businessmen: George Stacey Gibson of Saffron Walden, Smith Harrison of London, and James Reckitt of Hull.

Knitted pin balls such as these were often worked as gifts and keepsakes, sometimes to be sold. Pins were expensive items and for as long as embroidery had existed pincushions had been made and traded.

Written By The King Of Prussia.
At Breslaw

Love By Hope Is Still Sustained
Zeal By The Reward Thats Gained
In Power Authority Begins
Weakness Strength From Prudence Wins
Honesty Is Credits Wealth
Temperance The Support Of Health
Joys From Calm Contentment Spring
Content Is Competence That King
Competence As You May See
Springs From Good Oconomy
Maids To Fan A Lovers Fire
Sweetness More Than Charms Require
Authors More From Truth May Gain
Than From Tropes That Please The Vain
Arts Will Less Than Virtues Tend
Happiness And Life To Blend
He That Happiness Would Get
Prudence More Must Prize Than Wit
More Than Riches Rosy Health
Blameless Quiet More Than Wealth
Nought To Owe And Nought To Hoar
Little Land And Little Board
Little Favourite True And Kind
These Are Blessings To My Mind
I When Winter Comes Desire
Little Room But Plenteous Fire
Temperate Glasses Generous Wine
Dishes Few Whenever I Dine
Yes My Sober Thoughts Are Such
Man Must Never Have Too Much
Not Too Much What Solid Sense
Three Such Little Words Dispense
Too Much Rest Benumbs The Mind
Too Much Strife Distracts Mankind
Too Much Negligence Is Sloth
Too Much Zeal Is Follys Graeth
Too Much Love Our Peace Annoys
Too Much Physic Life Destroys
Too Much Cunning Is Fraud Full Art
Too Much Firmness Want Of Heart
Too Much Sparing Makes A Knave
Those Are Rash That Are Too Brave
Too Much Weight Like Wealth Oppress
Too Much Fame With Care Distresses
Too Much Pleasure Death Will Bring
Too Much Wives A Dangerous Thing
Too Much Truth Is Follys Guide
Too Much Spirit Is But Pride
He Is A Dupe That Is Too Free
Too Much Bounty Weak Much Be
Too Much Complaisance A Knave
Too Much Zeal To Please A Slave
This Too Much Though Bad It Seem
Changed With Ease Too Good You'll
But In This You Are My Friends
For On Trifles All Depends
Trifles Often Turn The Scale
When In Love Or Law We Fail
Trifles To The Great Commend
Trifles Make Proud Beauty Bend
Trifles Prompt The Poets Strain
Trifles Oft Distract The Brain
Trifles Trifles More Or Less
Give Us Or With Hold Success
Trifles When We Hope Can Cheer
Trifles Hurt Us When We Fear
All The Flames That Lovers Know
Trifles Quench And Trifles Blow

Ah Ye Who Meet Stern Winters Frown
Upheld By Fortunes Power Ful Hand
Who See The Chilling Snow Come Do[wn]
With All Her Comforts At Command
1
O Think Of Their Less Happy Doom
Whom Povertys Sharp Woes Assail
No Sparkling Fire No Chearful Room
Revive Their Cheek Cold Sunk And Pale
2
Deep Howls The Wind The Pelting Rain
Drips Through The Shattered Casement Co[ld]
While The Sad Mothers Arms Contain
Her Infants Shivering In Their Fold
3
In Vain They Raise Their Piteous Cry
And Plead At Hungry Natures Call
Their Only Food A Mothers Sigh
Their Only Warmth The Tears That Fall
4
Stretchd On His Miserable Bed
The Wretched Father Sinks In Grief
Pale Sickness Rests Upon His Head
And Only Hopes From Death Relief
5
The Parents Tender Mournful Eyes
Mingle Their Faint And Humid Beams
Fresh Woes From Retrospection Rise
Fresh Source From Mercys Fountain
6
O Rich The Transport Might Be Thine
To Soothe Their Sufferings Into Peace
To Bid The Sun Of Comfort Shine
And Wants Oppressive Empire Cease
7
To See The Glow Of Health Return
Reanimate Then Faded Cheek
Lifes Feeble Spark Rekindled Burn
And Give What Language Cannot Spea[k]
8
On Fancys Pinions Oft I Room
With Pity Partner Of My Flight
Forget A While That Griefs My Own
And Taste A Soothing Sweet Delight
9
Forget The Many Poignant Woes rth
That Weigh This Drooping Form To E[arth]
Where Restless Sorrow Hopes Repose
Scapd From Those Ills Which Gave It
10
O Ye Embarked For Pleasures Shore
Restrain A While The Fluttering Sail
At Pitys Call Retard The Oar
Nor Let Her Plaintive Pleadings Fail
11
Anne Jennings Wrought This Sampl[er]

When All Thy Mercies O My God
My Rising Soul Surveys
Transported With The View I Am Lost
In Wonder Love And Praise
O How Shall Words With Equal Warmth
The Gratitude Declare
That Glows Within My Ravished Heart
But Thou Canest Read It There
2
Thy Providence My Life Sustained
And All My Wants Redressed
When In The Silent Womb I Lay
And Hung Upon The Breast
3
To All My Weak Complaints And Cries
Thy Mercy Lent An Ear
Ere Yet My Feeble Thoughts Had Learned
To Form Themselves In Prayer
4
Unnumbered Comforts To My Soul
Thy Tender Care Bestowed
Before My Infant Heart Conceived
From Whom These Comforts Flowed
5
When In The Slippery Paths Of Youth
With Heedless Steps I Ran
Thine Arm Unseen Conveyed Me Safe
And Led Me Up To Man
6
Through Hidden Dangers Toils And Death
It Gently Cleared My Way
And Through The Pleasing Snares Of Vice
More To Be Feared Than They
7
When Worn With Sickness Oft Hast Thou
With Health Renewed My Face
And When In Sins And Sorrows Sunk
Revived My Soul With Grace
8
Thy Bounteous Hand With Worldly Bliss
Has Made My Cup Run Over
And In A Kind And Faithful Friend
Has Doubled All My Store
9
Ten Thousand Thousand Precious Gifts
My Daily Thanks Employ
Nor Is The Least A Chearful Heart
That Tastes Those Gifts With Joy
10
Through Every Period Of My Life
Thy Goodness Ill Pursue
And After Death In Distant Worlds
The Glorious Theme Renew
11
When Nature Fails And Day And Night
Divide Thy Works No More
My Ever Grateful Heart O Lord
Thy Mercy Shall Adore
12
Through All Eternity To Thee
A Joyful Song Ill Raise
For Oh Eternitys Too Short
To Utter All Thy Praise
13

Anne Jennings Wrough This Sampler
By The Directions Of Mistress Parker
School Mistress In The Orphan School
Near Calcutta In Bengal East Indias

Chapter Four

SAMPLERS OF THE POOR

PRIOR to the seventeenth century, only a very few schools were specifically founded to educate the female children of the poor, notably Christ's Hospital School, whose doors opened to accept 'fatherless and pore men's mayden children' in 1553. However, perhaps due to the spread of Puritan values during the Stuart period or simply because of an increase in the numbers of men and women who could afford to endow charity schools, the education of the poor was increasingly being addressed. Whilst educational opportunities remained limited for the children of the poor, female or male, there was certainly an increase in the number of charity schools being founded during the seventeenth century.

An early example was the foundation of the Red Maids' School in Bristol. In 1634 the common council of Bristol set up a committee to 'consider of a meet woman with twelve young girles to be settled for a begining in the new hospital of Mr Alderman Whitsons gifte'. After giving financial aid to Bristol Grammar and the Cathedral School, wealthy merchant John Whitson left in his will the funds for what became known as the 'Red Maids' School', initially educating twelve girls in the subjects of singing, reading, and sewing. The girls were accepted between eight and ten years of age and their keep was paid for by the proceeds of the sale of their needlework.[31] Some time later, in 1698, the Society for Promoting Christian Knowledge (SPCK) was founded with the specific aim of setting up schools for the poor both at home and in the colonies.

In 1709 the founding committee of the Blue Coats School in Ipswich issued a list of requirements for the position of Schoolmistress. It stated that she had to be:

> of good life and Character above the age of Thirty Years one whose Affection has been constantly to ye Worship and Communion of ye Church of England as by Law established Who can Read well, of Prudence to manage youth, and of competent Knowledge in the Principals of ye Christian religion according to ye doctrine of ye Church of England as by law established, &able to instruct her Scholars therein. And also a good Workwoman that she may Teach scholars the Use of their Needles in all Necessary and useful housewifely sorts of plain work, & knitting.[32]

Whilst we know from contemporary records that needlework was an important part of the curriculum of seventeenth-century charity schools the author knows of no surviving seventeenth-century samplers that can positively be attributed to a named charity school. The practice of naming schools on samplers is, however,

Opposite: The sampler worked by Anne Jennings under the direction of Mistress Parker is one of a number known to have been worked at this institution in Calcutta. The other known examples are housed in the collection of the Metropolitan Museum in New York, and all bear striking similarities.

73

This poignant sampler worked at St Clement Danes Charity School is one of a small group of samplers known to have been worked at this school. They all share many common features although this is the earliest dated.

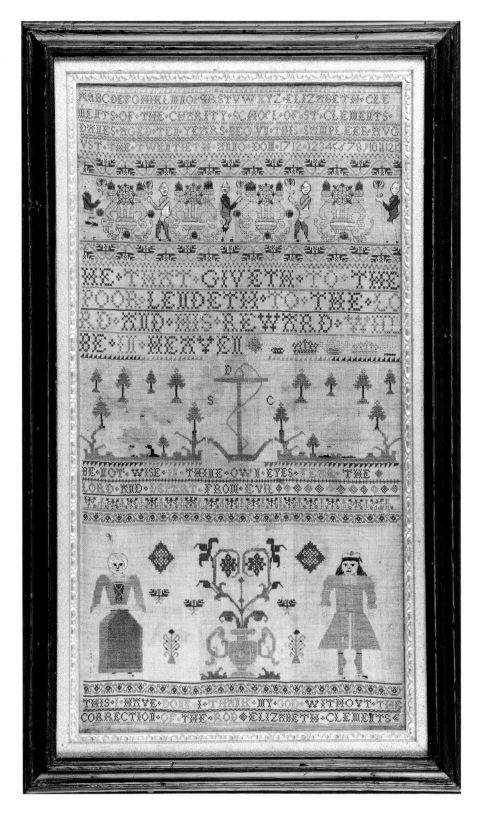

extremely rare in this period and so it is perhaps unsurprising that this should be the case. It is not until the eighteenth century, when the naming of individual schools on samplers becomes slightly more usual, that we find the earliest example of a sampler that we can positively attribute to a charity school.

The sampler by Elizabeth Clements, dated 1712, was worked at the charity school of St Clement Danes, the girls' school founded in 1702 in the City of Westminster (a boys' school had been founded in the previous year). This sampler is at present the earliest recorded named sampler worked at this charity school. The bands of lettering and numerals on this sampler are typical of the period, although the band of boxer figures harks back to the seventeenth century. The inscription 'This I have done I thank my God without the / correction of the rod' hints at the strict discipline that prevailed in the charity schools of this period. It is believed that the two figures illustrated in period dress towards the bottom of the sampler represent the schoolmaster and mistress.[33]

The foundation of charity schools, orphanages, asylums, and hospital schools continued to gather momentum throughout the eighteenth century. These institutions were either founded by religious groups eager to expand their sphere of influence or by wealthy individuals who out of a pious belief felt that it was their

The sampler by Margaret Campbell is remarkably finely worked on a fine gauze ground in coloured silks. This sampler demonstrates that decorative designs and expensive materials were not always the preserve of the rich.

duty to show gratitude to God through charitable donations. These institutions placed great importance on the teaching of needlework as part of their curriculum, and it is from them that some of the finest examples of schoolgirl samplers survive.

One notable institution from which a substantial body of work survives is that set up by Henry Raine. Henry Raine lived in Wapping, East London, between 1679 and 1738, where he had made a fortune out of brewing. A pious churchman, he decided to settle some of his wealth on a variety of charitable causes. He opened his first school in 1717 to accommodate, clothe and educate fifty boys and fifty girls in a newly erected building known as Raine's House. The school was to be run by a schoolmaster and mistress who were to instruct the children in the Christian religion and other subjects conducive to the future of their charges. In 1736, Raine's Asylum or Hospital, a charity boarding school for forty girls, was established close by. After completing their elementary education at Raine's House, the girls moved to the new institution where they were trained by a matron, with the objective of going into service. A condition of entry was that the parents agreed to relinquish to the trustees the placing of their daughters in suitable positions on completing their four years of further education.

The school gained the nickname 'the hundred pound school' from its practice of providing two marriage portions a year to former pupils who could prove that both they and their future husbands were of good character and both practising members of the Church of England. On 1 May and 26 December each year, up to six candidates would draw lots from a casket for the two marriage settlements of £100 each plus £5 for a wedding feast, hence the nickname.[34]

In the wake of the rapid industrialisation of the nineteenth century, which was shaping not only the British economy but also changing the social fabric of the countryside, the traditional agricultural economy was being eroded and many of the dispossessed rural populations were moving to the cities. This coincided with a rapid expansion in the general population, rising from approximately 10.4 million in 1801 to 18.5 million by 1841. Much of this growing population was crowded into the newly developing urban ghettos, where factory workers were faced with poor sanitation and little or no social welfare provision.

There were of course those who benefited from the Industrial Revolution, making vast fortunes; the skilled labourers without whom this expansion would not have been possible were much in demand, many being able to rise from the ranks of the manual workforce, and join the growing ranks of the middle classes. The demand for education amongst the middle ranks of society was satiated by the growing number of

The price list of the charges to be levied on plain sewing taken in by the Cheltenham Female Orphan School. Money was often raised by the authorities of charitable institutions in just such a manner.

A LIST OF THE PRICES FOR PLAIN WORK
Done at the Cheltenham Female Orphan Asylum & Old School of Industry.

	s	d.	to	s	d.		s	d.	to	s	.
Fine Shirt .... fr.	1	6	:	2	6	Pinafore, with sleeves fr.	0	3	:	0	6
Ditto trimmed ....—	2	6	:	3	6	Muslin Handkerchief —	0	1	:	0	3
Shirt of inferior cloth —		8	:	1	6	Pocket ditto ...... —	0	½	:	0	1½
Boy's fine Shirt .... —		9	:	1	0	French Cambric ditto —	0	1½	:	0	2
Ditto trimmed .... —	1	0	:	1	8	Collar & pr. wristbands —	0	3	:	0	6
Ditto of inferior cloth —		6	:	1	0	Ditto, fine .... —	0	4	:	0	8
Fine Shift .... —		10	:	1	10	Coarse Sheets, per pr. —	0	8	:	1	0
Ditto trimmed .... —	2	0	:	2	3	Fine ditto .... —	1	0	:	1	4
Shift of inferior cloth —		7	:	1	0	Ditto of 3 breadths —	1	6	:	2	6
Night Shift ...... —	1	0	:	1	8	Pillow Cases, per pr. —	0	3	:	0	6
Ditto trimmed .... —	1	6	:	3	6	Table Cloth ...... —	0	2	:	1	0
Child's Shift ..... —		4	:	1	0	Towels, per dozen .. —	0	6	:	1	3
Night Cap, plain .. —		4	:	0	10	Dusters, per dozen .. —	0	4	:	0	8
Ditto, double borders —	1	0	:	1	6	Hemming, per yard —	0	½	:	0	1
Calico Dressing Gown —		6	:	2	0	Seaming, per yard .. —	0	½	:	0	1
Plain Petticoat .... —		6	:	0	10	Backstitching, per yd. —	0	¾	:	0	1½
Pockets, per pair .. —		4	:	0	8	Tucking, per yard .. —	0	½	:	0	1
Apron .... —		2	:	0	4	Marking, per letter —	0	¼	:	0	0½
Tippet .... —		2	:	0	6	Ditto, per figure .... —	0	¼	:		0
Pinafore .... —		2	:	0	5	Knitting, per ounce —	0	2	:		3

BABY LINEN.

	s	d.	to	s	d.		s	d.	to	s	d.
Shirt .... —	0	2			4	Plain Robe ...... —	0	8	:	1	6
Cap .... —	0	3	:		0	Bed Gown .... —	0	6	:	1	0
Night Cap .... —	0	2			6	Petticoat .... —	0	6	:	1	0
Flannel .... —	0	3		1	0	Pinafore .... —	0	2	:	0	4

☞ *The charges between the limits will be regulated by the size and pattern of the work and the fineness of the materials.—It is requested that work sent may be* CUT OUT *with the* GREATEST EXACTNESS, *and a list be sent with it, also the name and residence of the person to whom the work belongs.—A bill will be given when the work is returned; and it is requested that the amount be paid at the time.*

An extra charge for work not cut out.

VOL. II. D

private schools, public schools and grammar schools, whereas for the vast majority of the poor there was very little provision. The conditions of the working classes, their health and educational provision became a major consideration, not just of the Government but of the Church, welfare organisations, and conscientious individuals who set up institutions to cater for those needs. Much of the educational provision provided by charitable institutions offered little more than Bible reading and practical instruction. Hannah Moore, the well-known educationalist, wrote of the education offered at one of her schools: 'My plan of instruction is extremely simple and limited. They learn on weekdays such coarse works as may fit them for servants. I allow of no writing for the poor…'[35]

Work survives from many institutions too numerous to name individually from throughout the nineteenth century, but the examples illustrated in these pages demonstrate just how fine much of the work produced in such institutions was. For many of these young girls the chance of going into service would undoubtedly have been far more appealing than life in a factory or down the mines. The samplers and other needlework they produced would have served two main purposes: firstly the sale of their work would have provided for their keep, and secondly it would have provided a *curriculum vitae* for their future employers, a method of demonstrating the skills necessary for the marking of household linen, darning and mending, all requirements of a life in service.

Interestingly a list of prices exists for the plain work undertaken at the 'Cheltenham Female Orphan Asylum School of Industry' where the small pincushion was worked. This pincushion, along with the sampler worked at the same institution, demonstrates the level of skill required by the institution. The fact that so far no signed work from this institution has come to light may be to do with the idea of modesty – or it may simply be that these too were intended for sale. In 1806 the stated purpose of the orphanage was:

> To clothe, maintain and educate female orphans and other female children of the poor. To inculcate into their tender minds such principals of religion and morality, to rescue them from the contamination of idleness and vice and train them up in the habit of industrious and cheerful obedience, by instructing them in such kinds of housework as may qualify them for servants in respectable families.[36]

The pocket sampler worked by Susannah Carter and dated 1800 again shows the very fine nature of the work that these girls were expected to produce. Pocket samplers along with watch holders and covers, pincushions, miniature pillows and bags were all worked in orphanages and asylums, and often (as in this case) state that they were worked within such institutions. It is also not uncommon to find the verses worked on them alluding to the plight of orphans. Compare the verse worked

Pincushion worked at the Cheltenham Female Orphan Asylum School of Industry. This is one of several surviving examples from this institution.

Cheltenham
Female Orphan Asylum
Founded By
Her Late Most Gracious Majesty
Queen Charlotte
1806
And Patronized By
Her Most Gracious Majesty
Queen Victoria
1842

ABCDEFGHIJKLMNOPQRSTUVWXYZ&
abcdefghijklmnopqrstuvwxyz1234567891Q

Religion is our guide
and Industry
our Support

When my Father and my Mother forsake me
the Lord taketh me up

This sampler is one of several examples worked at this school. It is interesting that none of the examples that do survive is named. A number of acrostic samplers also survive from Cheltenham, probably intended to be made up into pincushions and sold.

on the anonymous pocket sampler, illustrated on page 79, with that on Susannah Carter's pocket sampler.

There is one institution that cannot go unmentioned, and that is Bristol Orphanage. The orphan houses of Bristol were founded by George Muller, a German independent minister and philanthropist who came to England in 1829. He opened the first orphanage in the St Paul's area of Bristol, in 1836, taking in thirty girls. The cholera epidemic that ravaged Bristol around this date resulted in a high death rate amongst the population and left many children orphaned. In response to the demand Muller purchased land at Ashley Down on the outskirts of Bristol where a second orphanage was built. Not content, Muller went on to build four more orphanages and by 1870 they could take in just over 2,000 children.

Discipline was strict and the orphans had to share the work necessary for the smooth running of the institution. Girls worked in the laundry and kitchens whilst boys worked in the gardens. Children of both sexes were taught to sew and knit. The Bristol orphanages became widely known and received much publicity, prompting visits from well-known people such as Charles Dickens. Bristol kept very full records of the children who passed through its doors: the children's next of kin was recorded as was the name and address of their first employer, including the capacity in which they worked. The reasons for their admission and who admitted them were also recorded. It is an interesting fact that many of the orphans came very considerable distances, often admission being arranged by missionaries working in deprived communities. No subscription was required for admission, which was entirely free of charge; the orphanage worked on the principles of Muller's personal belief that all needs would be met by God as a direct result of prayer, and in this Muller seems to have met with much success.

It is the large surviving body of work that makes Bristol an important institution in terms of the history of sampler making. The samplers themselves form a highly recognisable group, almost always worked in red cotton thread onto a white or ecru cotton ground. Typically the samplers allow for very little wasted space and are densely worked with rows of different alphabets, numerals and border patterns. The inclusion of an image of the Bible is almost universal and is significant as every child was given a Bible on leaving the orphanage. The workmanlike appearance of the samplers is clearly the result of their purpose as a reference for the girl's needle skills. From an examination of a number of Bristol orphanage samplers it would seem that the very densely worked samplers were generally worked when the girls were about fifteen or sixteen years of age. The two samplers worked by Florence

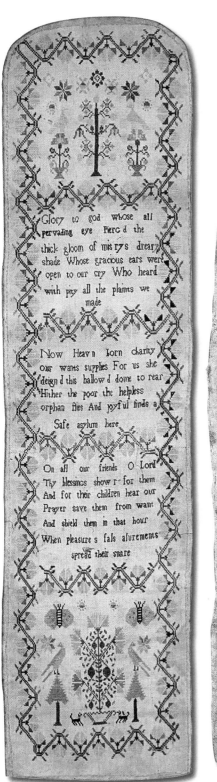

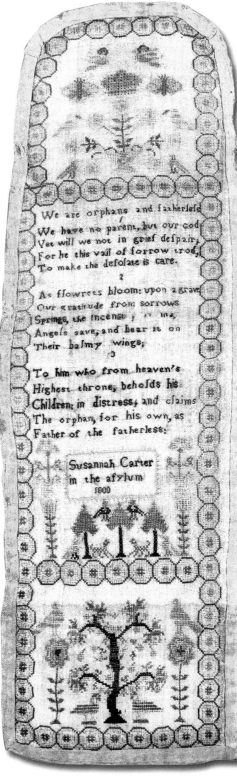

Glory to god whose all
pervading eye Pierc'd the
thick gloom of mis'rys dreary
shade Whose gracious ears were
open to our cry Who heard
with pity all the plaints we
made

Now Heav'n born charity
Our wants supplies For us she
deign'd this hallow'd dome to rear
Hither the poor the helpless
orphan flies And joyful finds a
Safe asylum here

On all our friends O Lord
Thy blessings show'r for them
And for their children hear our
Prayer save them from want
And shield them in that hour
When pleasure's fals alurements
spread their snare

We are orphans and fatherless
We have no parent, but our god
Yet will we not in grief despair,
For he this vail of sorrow trod,
To make the desolate is care.

2
As fflowrets bloom: upon a grave
Our gratitude from sorrows
Springs, the incense ; . . . .
Angels save, and bear it on
Their balmy wings;
3
To him who from heaven's
Highest throne, beholds his
Children; in distress, and claims
The orphan, for his own, as
Father of the fatherless;

Susannah Carter
in the asylum
1800

Far left: This
anonymous sampler
pocket is typical of
many worked in
orphanages and
asylums across
England. Often
worked with strongly
moralistic verses, they
tell us a lot about
the attitude to
charity and the
education of the poor.

Left: The moralistic
verse on Susannah
Carter's pocket,
worked at about
the same time as the
anonymous pocket
illustrated, provides
an example of the
importance of God
in late eighteenth-
and early nineteenth-
century society.

79

The samplers worked at Bristol Orphanage are possibly the best known group of any orphanage work. They were known for their dense working, so it was clear that economy was important.

Lancastle in 1887 and 1888 are worked to a larger scale and are far less densely arranged, which may be accounted for by her slightly younger age of thirteen and fourteen when she worked these examples.[37]

The Sunday School movement pioneered by Robert Raikes (1735–1811) was highly influential in contributing to educational policy during the nineteenth century. Born in Gloucester, Robert Raikes inherited a publishing business from his father, becoming proprietor of the *Gloucester Journal* in 1755. His ownership of the paper became a useful tool in his later philanthropic work. Raikes, through his involvement with the inmates of the local jail (most of whom were incarcerated under the Poor Law) felt that vice would be better tackled by prevention than cure. He saw education as the best route to this end, forming the opinion that the best time for schooling would be on a Sunday so that employment opportunities would not be jeopardised.

It is rare to find more than one name on a sampler worked at Bristol, and this example does not appear to be the work of more than one hand. It could be a friendship sampler since the girls, although originating from different parts of the country, were the same age.

Below left and right: The two samplers worked by Florence Lancastle in successive years are relatively simple by Bristol standards. Many of the samplers worked at Bristol were worked by slightly older girls, which could account for this slightly simplified composition.

Above and below: These two samplers worked at Bennett Street Sunday School in 1841 and 1846 provide a valuable record not just of the school itself but of the costs involved in its foundation. Bennett Street was one of the largest Sunday schools in the country and at its peak it was teaching over 4,000 pupils.

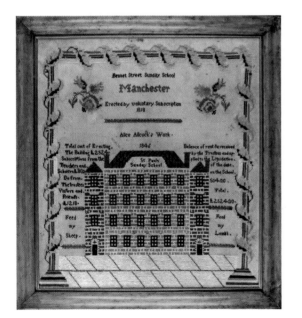

He started his first school in around 1780 in Sooty Alley, Gloucester, for the children of chimney sweeps, and publicised it through the pages of his newspaper. Very quickly his ideas gained momentum and by 1783 a number of schools had opened in and around Gloucester. In 1785 the Sunday School Society was founded to coordinate and organise his ideas. Initially there was some derision of Raikes's ideas: it was felt a desecration of the Sabbath by some Christians, and fears were expressed about educating the poor above their station (the schools were sometimes referred to as 'Raikes's ragged schools'). However, encouraged by the support received by Raikes's followers – namely Sarah Trimmer and Hannah Moore, both of whom wrote moral tales for the young – his ideas spread rapidly, and by 1831 Sunday schools in Great Britain were ministering to 1,250,000 children every week, approximately a quarter of the child population.[38]

Wherever Sunday Schools are established instead of seeing the
Streets filled on the Sabbath day with ragged children engaged
In idle sports, uttering oaths and blasphemies, we behold them
Assembled in school, neat in appearance and apparel and
Receiving with the greatest attention instruction given suited to
Their capacities and conditions.'[39]

Bennett Street Sunday School, Manchester, where the two illustrated samplers were worked, was founded around 1800 by David Stott. First known as Stott's School, it first occupied premises in Gun Street and Primrose Street but in 1818 a new building was erected in Bennett Street and paid for by public subscription. Religious instruction was the school's primary function and the children were taught to read by studying the Bible. They were, however, not taught to write, an indication of which is given in Hannah's sampler:

Oh Praise the Lord A change is Wrought
At Sabbath School I have Been Taught
To Read The Bible Book Divine
And Make its Blessed Contents Mine

Three Sunday schools were run under the same establishment in the St Paul's district of Manchester and were by 1820 ministering to the needs of over

4,000 children. Alice Allcock's work leaves an interesting historical record by stating the costs involved in erecting the school building, the various subscriptions and the balances of the rent.[40]

Although the two illustrated punishment samplers are believed to have been used in the nursery at Holkham Hall, Norfolk, they are of a type which could have been worn at many of the charity schools throughout the country. Various devices including arm bands, dunces' caps, and placards were used during the nineteenth century as methods of correction with the intention of shaming the offender. A reference to punishment at the Blue Coat Charity School, Christ's Hospital, Hertfordshire, records:

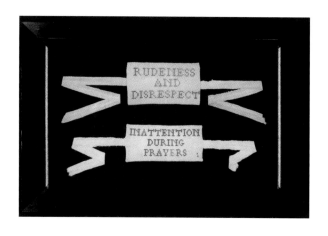

This rare surviving pair of punishment samplers is believed to have been used in the nursery at Holkham Hall in Norfolk. They are, however, typical of those used at many schools during this period.

> Punishments which made an example of the offender in the eyes of her school fellows, and held her up to scorn or ridicule, were frequent. For this purpose, a liar had a red tongue, cut out of flannel, hung round her neck; a pilferer had to suffer a broad linen band to be tied around her forehead on which were emblazoned in cross stitch the awful words, 'BEWARE THE THIEF'; whilst those who had lapsed into lesser moral sin had similar bands labelled 'GOSSIP' tied around their heads.[41]

In Charlotte Bronte's novel *Jane Eyre* we have another graphic insight into the life of boarders at a charity school. The vivid descriptions of the Lowood Institution include the wearing of placards as a punishment:

> Next morning, Miss Scratcherd wrote in conspicuous characters on a piece of paste board the word 'SLATTERN' and bound it like a phylactery round Helen's large, mild and benign looking forehead. She wore it till evening....

A selection of punishment bands, including two bands identical to the ones illustrated here, are held in Christ's Hospital Museum in Horsham, West Sussex.

The founding of charity schools was not confined to Great Britain. Many charity schools were founded in the British colonies, and although quite rare, surviving samplers from the colonies prove that often the curriculum followed was very similar to the curriculum offered back home.

The sampler that opens this chapter is by Anne Jennings and worked 'By The Direction of Mistress Parker / School Mistress in the Orphan School / Near Calcutta in Bengal East Indias'. It dates from the end of the eighteenth century. Although this example is undated, we can ascribe an approximate date based on a group of samplers also worked under the direction of Mistress Parker in Bengal and dated 1797. From research undertaken on Anne Jennings we know that she married a Richard Walker in 1796, so her sampler clearly predates this event.

The British in India towards the end of the eighteenth century were facing something of a social crisis. Many of the largely male population had come over to India with the military, or as employees of the East India Company, or as Government employees working for the various administrative institutions necessary to the colony. Relatively few women ventured to make the often dangerous passage and, of those that did, many were considered to be of dubious morality and therefore unsuitable as marriage material. Consequently many of the British men in India had formed relationships with Indian or Eurasian women. Whilst there is evidence of marriages between the races, many relationships were never formalised; none the less the population of Eurasian children had grown very rapidly by the end of the eighteenth century. A high death rate amongst the adult British male population led to a large number of orphaned children.

> Of all the covenanted civil servants the best-off amongst the British and most able to care for their health, who went out to India between 1762 and 1771 only one in ten had managed to return to Britain by 1784. Almost half had died in India. Many of them died young and poor, leaving their children in need.[42]

For the ruling British society in India this posed a problem. Perhaps due in part to a philanthropic desire to inculcate these children with the values of contemporary Britain, and also perhaps due to a genuine paternal desire to see them included in British society, attention was turned to providing for the needs of these children.

Whilst the need for provision had been recognised at the beginning of the eighteenth century, by the middle of the century it was clear that the existing establishments were inadequate for the increasing demand. A rapid expansion in the foundation of both military and civil orphanages took place from the 1780s onwards, catering for the increasing numbers of the children of the poor British and Eurasian population, many of whom were military children.

Edina Christian's small mission school sampler is stitched in both English and a local dialect. It is likely that Edina was of mixed or Indian race and was converted to the Christian faith by the missionaries.

The Bengal Military Orphan Society had founded the Upper Military Orphanage in 1783 for the sons and daughters of officers, and in 1784 founded the Lower Military Orphanage at Alipore in which the sons and daughters of soldiers and non-commissioned officers were housed. In all three presidencies (Calcutta, Madras and Bombay), many different organisations founded orphanages. Much as in Britain, the level of education received depended on the social class from which the children came. Girls in general received less education than the boys, most being prepared for marriage or a life in service. The daughters of the non-commissioned officers and soldiers were taught basic literacy and arithmetic skills

This anonymous missionary sampler is worked in Malayalam, a language related to Tamil. It is likely to have been worked at a church missionary school. The samplers worked at these schools bear testament to the evangelical zeal that drove these early missionaries.

and the needlework skills necessary to procure a job in service or to support themselves in trade. The daughters of the officers received a better education but also received instruction in needlework and embroidery. If these girls were to find a husband from the officer class, social accomplishments were considered particularly important.

Free schools and mission schools further expanded the provision for the children of the poor. A Free School at Calcutta was founded in 1789 and merged with the

It is unusual, but not unheard of, to find stitched letters. Although the young Betsy states she cannot write to Mrs Wilson, she clearly has good knowledge of words. It was believed by many that writing should not be taught to the children of the poor.

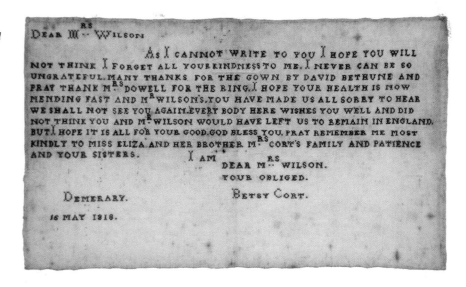

earlier Charity School in 1800. By 1818 it boarded 189 boys and 87 girls as well as educating 36 day boys. Civil orphanages for boys and girls were opened in Madras in 1807 and 1810 respectively. At Bombay, the Society for the Education of the Poor was founded in 1815, expanding the capacity of the original Charity School. By 1817 it was educating 83 boys and 46 girls and had a 'long list of children waiting for admission as soon as funds will allow.'[43]

Many of these institutions had strict admission policies with European children often having priority; 'the next in preference are country-born children of mixed race, whose situation renders them objects of great pity'.[44] Admissions policies were often based on the eighteenth-century judgement of who was most deserving, with the illegitimate children of mixed liaisons often coming at the bottom of the admissions ladder.

The many mission schools took children regardless of race, providing they were Christians or ready converts. The SPCK had been founding schools as early as the mid eighteenth century; the schools were usually attached to the local church and funded by them. Perhaps the young Edina Christian, who worked the sampler illustrated, was so named because of her religious conversion. The text of this sampler is worked in cross stitch and uses both the English language and a local dialect, indicating that Edina was probably of mixed race.

The sampler illustrated on page 85 is from the south of India, and is worked with a text in a local dialect, Malayalam, a language related to Tamil. Research tells us that this sampler was almost certainly worked at a school founded by the Church Missionary Society established at Kottayam (Kerala) at the beginning of the nineteenth century. The Reverend Henry Baker, who founded the society together with his wife, established a number of schools in the remote forested hills of southern India around the area he named Herons' Pool. The schools were part of a systematic evangelical programme specifically aimed at the conversion of non-Christian locals. It is interesting that many of the motifs that appear on this sampler are striking in their similarity to the motifs appearing on English samplers of the period.[45]

Although possibly not worked in an institution, the letter worked by Betsy Cort in 1818 serves to demonstrate one of the uses to which needle skills could be put. Such embroidered letters are extremely rare but do record an aspect of life in the colonies. It is believed that Mrs Wilson was a missionary in Demerara in the early nineteenth century. The young Betsy's relationship to her is unclear, but her reference to being unable to write indicates that she was educated at one of the missionary schools. Just as was the convention in England, young girls were taught to read but were often not taught to write.

This exceptionally rare hair sampler was worked by a notorious female prisoner, Annie Parker. Several samplers are known to have been worked by her during her many spells in various jails.

87

The exceptionally rare hair sampler worked by Annie Parker, whilst not worked in an orphanage, seems highly likely to be the work of a former orphan. The skill needed to work the minute stitches in human hair is almost incomprehensible to a modern viewer. The crocheted border, the choice of border patterns chosen, and the white work embroidery are all reminiscent of the type of work taught either in an orphanage or at a charity school. What is perhaps the most incredible aspect of this sampler is that it was worked in prison.

> The death has just taken place in Greenwich Union Infirmary of Annie Parker, aged 35, who has been over 400 times charged before the magistrates at Greenwich Police Court, with drunkenness but never with felony, and has spent the greater part of her life in prison. The cause of her death was consumption. She was always exceedingly well conducted in prison. She has a luxuriant head of hair and whilst in prison worked a number of samplers to give as gifts. These samplers were worked with her own hair, and are unbelievably fine …. Annie Parker was well educated and a bad word never escaped her. On one occasion a lady took her to Canada, with a view to her reformation, this failed as she could never refuse an intoxicating drink. On the morning of her death, she presented to a Dr Dixon, the assistant medical officer of the infirmary a laced edged sampler which was again worked with her own hair.[46]

Annie Parker is not the only known prisoner to have worked a sampler whilst in jail. Glasgow Museum has in its collection a particularly touching sampler signed only with the initials 'I. McK'. The verse reads:

I ENVY NOT VICTORIAS CROWN
ALL ALL HER GOLD IS VANITY
I AM HAPPIER IN MY LONELY CELL
THEN ANY qUEEN ON EARTH CAN BE
FOR GOLD NOR TREASURE HAVE I NONE
NO ONE ON EARTH TO CONVERSE WE
BUT I HAVE WHAT IS NOBLER STILL
THE KING OF qUEENS FOR COMPANY
DONE IN EXILE
BY I. McK

The reference to Queen Victoria clearly dates the sampler to after 1837, after Robert Peel had introduced his Prison Reform Bill of 1823, thus providing legislation to improve the conditions in Britain's jails. However, prison conditions remained harsh (debtors' prisons had been exempt from the legislation), causing luminaries such as Charles Dickens and Elizabeth Fry to comment publicly on the matter. Elizabeth Fry herself spent time visiting female prisoners in London, providing them with sewing materials in order to enable them either to gain employment when they reached their final destination or to have work to sell upon arrival.[47]

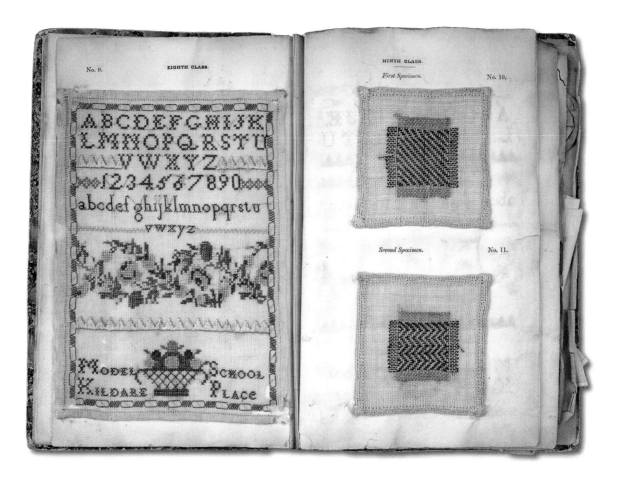

Pages displaying the work of Sarah Darby (1837) at the Model School established by the Kildare Place Society.

From the earliest years of the nineteenth century the establishment of charitable schools across Britain was to provide the foundation for the compulsory education enshrined in Forster's Education Act of 1870. The Society for Promoting the Education of the Poor in Ireland, which had grown out of the Sunday School movement, provides us with a prime example of the progression towards a state-funded education free and available to all. Also known as the Kildare Place Society, its headquarters located in Dublin, the society promoted improved teaching methods, advised on the design and construction of schools and produced a range of text books. In order to train teachers and demonstrate their teaching methods they founded a model school in Dublin in 1816 which consisted of two large school rooms, one for boys and one for girls. In 1831, Government funding of the society ceased, being replaced by a joint initiative between the state and local authorities based on the experience and practices developed by the Kildare Place Society. After a new education act was introduced by the Chief Secretary of Ireland, Edward Stanley, 14th Earl of Derby, commissioners were appointed and with part of the annual budget of £30,000 a new model school was opened in Dublin in 1835. It was proposed that 5,000 national or primary schools be opened across Ireland, with one model school established in each of the thirty-two counties. 'The objectives of these model schools were declared to be the promotion of united (i.e. integrated) education; improved methods of literary and scientific education; and the training of teachers.'

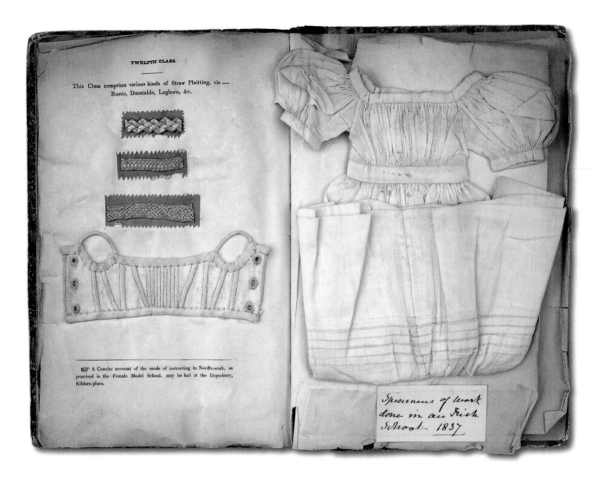

TWELFTH CLASS.

This Class comprises various kinds of Straw Plaitting, viz.—
Rustic, Dunstable, Leghorn, &c.

A Concise account of the mode of instructing in Needle-work, as practised in the Female Model School, may be had at the Depository, Kildare-place.

Specimens of work done in an Irish School 1837

Plain sewing included teaching all the skills necessary for garment production. Each class would teach a different skill and the girls would then assemble them into a pre-printed work book.

Opposite right: It is not uncommon to find examples of plain sewing which have become detached from their work books.

The model schools consisted of an infant school, and a male and female school; each had workrooms attached for manual instruction. As well as trained teachers, the schools made use of pupil teachers called 'monitors', with the teaching staff accommodated within the school buildings. The pages of the work book with examples of plain sewing stitched by Sarah Darby at the female model school in 1837 demonstrate the practices followed by the schools. Needlework lessons were divided into four divisions, division one being the lowest. Each division was divided into four classes with specimens of each class displayed in their work books.

The term 'plain sewing' refers to those practice pieces worked whilst acquiring the needlework skills necessary for making garments. Hemming, darning, patching and seaming were all taught as a possible means of self support and were considered essential for homemaking; they and were taught throughout the British Isles during the nineteenth century. Children as young as three were expected to be able at least to thread a needle, and whilst plain sewing is often associated with charitable institutions teaching the daughters of the poor, it is likely that girls from all backgrounds did some form of plain sewing, whether it be in the form of a sampler or simply making dolls' clothes or embroidering a handkerchief. It seems inconceivable that girls as young as seven could have produced some of the samplers that survive today without first acquiring a degree of proficiency with a needle.

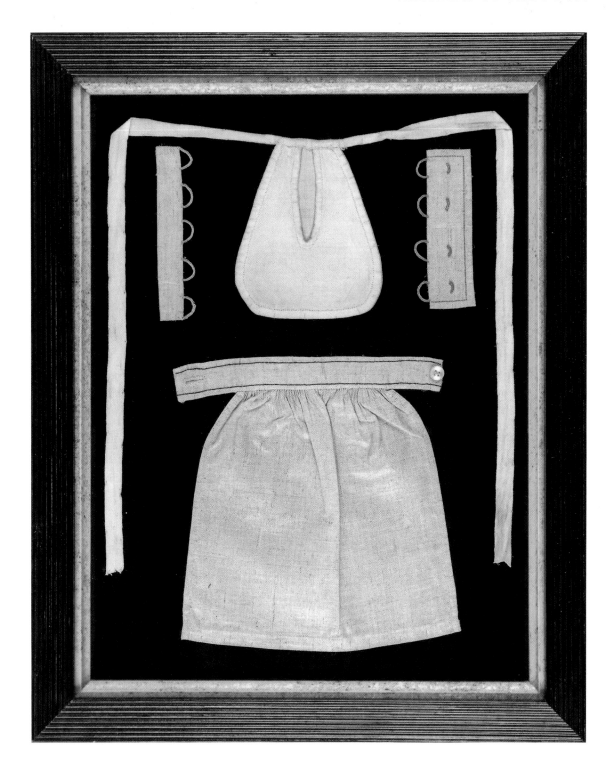

Next unto GOD dear Parents I address
Myself to you in humble thankfulness
For all your care & charge on me bestow'd
The means of learning unto me allow'd
Go on I pray and let me still pursue
Those golden arts the vulgar never knew

Anne Hillman finished
this in her 10 year 1808

Chapter Five

THE NINETEENTH CENTURY

Possibly the two most influential people in the story of education in the nineteenth century were Dr Andrew Bell and Joseph Lancaster. Dr Andrew Bell (1753–1832) was born in St Andrews, Scotland, and studied mathematics and natural philosophy in the local university. After a period working as a tutor in Virginia he returned to Britain following the American War of Independence, and he took up a position as a clergyman in the Church of England. Following a short period at the Episcopal Chapel in Leith, Bell took up a position as Chaplain to the East India Company in Madras, India. Whilst in India he worked at the Madras Male Orphan Asylum, which educated the children of soldiers. The lack of trained teachers caused Bell to develop a system whereby the older boys were instructed and they then instructed the younger boys. After his return to Britain in 1796, Bell wrote about his system of education in his publication *An Experiment in Education* (1797). During the nineteenth century Bell's 'Madras System' was adopted by Church of England schools throughout Britain and these were known as 'National' schools.[48]

Joseph Lancaster (1778–1838), a Quaker, was the son of a shopkeeper from Southwark, south London. In 1798 he founded a school in Borough Road, London, which worked on the same principles as those adopted by the Anglican National schools. During the first decade of the nineteenth century 'The Society for Promoting the Lancastrian System for the Education of the Poor' was created. The Lancastrian schools admitted children from the Nonconformist community and imposed a strict code of discipline. Although Lancaster had officially rejected the use of corporal punishment the harsh regime led the poet Robert Southey to write that 'despite his opposition to corporal punishment, he would rather be beaten than subjected to Lancastrian discipline'. Lancaster was eventually ejected from the society he had founded, when it was discovered that he had in fact inflicted corporal punishment on a number of boys whom he had taught. The society renamed itself 'The British and Foreign School Society' and enjoyed a period of great success, establishing many schools. Many samplers survive today worked in both National and British schools.[49]

Opposite: Anne Hillman's charming and colourful depiction of a family scene is one of two known, the other being in the Goodhart Collection housed at Montacute House in Somerset.

Mathematical samplers such as this example worked at the National School at Tunbridge Wells were intended to teach the girls the required skills necessary for keeping the household accounts. Frances was born in 1836, making it likely that the sampler dates from around the 1850s.

Left:Mathematical samplers such as this one worked at Sawston Girls' Board School, which had opened in 1876, combined the teaching of mathematics with plain sewing. Attendance was enforced at the growing number of board schools for children aged between five and ten.

Right: Esther Stewart's slave sampler with its striking image was worked two years before slavery was abolished in Britain and her colonies in 1838. The anti-slavery movement had become a powerful political force. Its leader in Parliament was William Wilberforce.

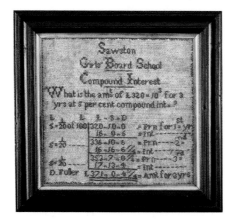

The majority of the surviving multiplication samplers which have been identified appear to have been worked in Scotland.

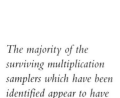

It was the Education Act of 1870 that introduced the modern system of education: it not only established a nationwide system of state education, but for the first time assured the existence of a dual system, with voluntary denominational and non-denominational state schools. The National and British schools founded by Bell and Lancaster were incorporated into this new state system. The Act required schools to be set up to supplement the existing schools already run by the Church, private individuals, and guilds. The country was divided into districts, and in those areas where there was a lack of provision school boards were to be established, responsible for raising the necessary funds to support the schools. The schools were often referred to as 'board schools'. The mathematical sampler illustrated demonstrates that the educational emphasis of these schools was shifting; needlework was not being taught simply for its own merit but was combining with subjects seen as increasingly necessary to equip children with the skills required by a modern society.

Mathematical samplers are relatively rare, but there is one group of mathematical samplers that is widely known. These seem to be almost exclusively Scottish in origin, but why this genre of sampler was worked most often in Scotland remains a mystery.

We associate the nineteenth century with the wealth that the Industrial Revolution brought to Great Britain – a century that saw tremendous growth in the size and affluence of the middle classes and a greater emphasis not only on the education of the poor but of their own daughters. The middle classes had never before had so much access to, and the means to buy, luxury manufactured goods, and so for many the necessity to produce household furnishings or the fashionable accessories of a comfortable life within the home had largely disappeared. A far greater proportion of the population could afford household staff, and what their servants could not produce or mend, they could purchase.

The traditional religious subjects found on the samplers of earlier centuries still prevailed. Adam and Eve and the

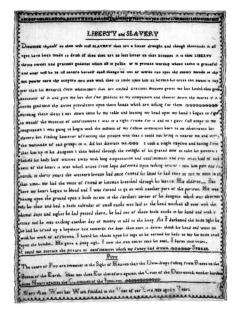

Spies from Canaan are often to be found, and representations of Solomon's Temple are amongst the most frequently worked of all subjects found on nineteenth-century samplers. But there is also evidence of a greater awareness of the political and social issues of the day. Esther Stewart and Mary Ann West both depict a knowledge of, and a sympathy towards the arguments surrounding the abolition of slavery. Esther worked her sampler with a bold depiction of a slave in chains based on an image designed originally as a medallion by Henry Webb, modelled by William Hackwood and made in Josiah Wedgwood's Etruria works in 1788. The political message of this image is reinforced with the inscription, 'AM I NOT A MAN AND A BROTHER', and had become the symbol for a campaign to abolish slavery. It is incidentally an image that is found on a number of samplers worked at Ackworth School. Mary Ann West's sampler worked in 1828 has in contrast a passage taken from Sterne on 'Liberty and Slavery'.

Awareness of important political reforms is in evidence in Rachel Bailey's interesting sampler, which reproduces the response of King George III to Lord Grenville on the subject of the 1807 Catholic Bill. The knowledge of historical events and the personalities that shaped them was not only taught in school but would have been disseminated throughout society by the circulation of an increasing number of newspapers and journals. Images of famous individuals, particularly military heroes, were frequently published in such papers and it is perhaps from just such a source that the two samplers of Field Marshal Suwarrow and the Duke of Brunswick were taken.

Nineteenth-century society was also not averse to celebrating its industrial, scientific and artistic achievements. The Great Exhibition of 1851 was widely acclaimed and prints of the Crystal Palace built to house the exhibition appeared

Left: Mary Ann West chose to copy a passage from Sterne about 'Liberty and Slavery'. It seems likely that she came from a politically aware reforming background. The twelve-man Committee for the Abolition of the African Slave Trade, set up in London in 1787, consisted of Quakers, dissenters and evangelical Anglicans.

Right: Religious subjects were favoured, with the majority coming from the Old Testament. A small number of very similar examples closely related to this one appear to have been worked under the same direction.

Right: Sampler recording the career of Field Marshal Suwarrow. It is probable that this sampler was worked from a printed source, probably published in one of the newspapers or journals of the period.

Far right: The Duke of Brunswick was an important political and military figure of the mid eighteenth century. He was married to Princess Augusta, the sister of George III of England, and so was well known in England and certainly featured in the history curriculum taught in many schools of the period.

Rachel Bailey's unusual political sampler worked in 1827 records the Catholic Bill introduced by Lord Grenville, which received an enormous amount of publicity in the early nineteenth century and clearly was the subject of conversation and lessons for the young Rachel.

everywhere (quite clearly these illustrations had not escaped Mary Ann Shead). The growth of the rail network and improvement of transport links was vital to the growth of the nineteenth-century Industrial Revolution and the wealth of Britain. The sense of pride in its many architectural accomplishments is in evidence in Mary Smallwood's sampler, with its depiction of the grand suspension bridge over the Menai Straits, linking Anglesey to the mainland.

Just as in the seventeenth and eighteenth centuries, death was never far away. Nineteenth-century samplers often record both awareness and an acceptance of the reality of life. Many of the verses found on nineteenth-century samplers make specific reference to the fleeting nature of life and the imminence of death.

> There is an hour when I must die.
> Nor can I tell how soon twill come.
> A thousand children young as I,
> Are calld by death to hear their doom.[50]

In no other genre of sampler is the awareness of life and death more apparent than in the family registers, on which it became fashionable to work in the nineteenth

The Great Exhibition attracted enormous publicity, and fuelled an upsurge in national pride. Over six million people, or one third of the population, had visited the Exhibition by the time it closed.

A representation of the new bridge over the Menai Straits by Mary Smallwood, worked in 1833.

century. Of the ten children born to John and Alice Chorlton six had died before reaching their sixth birthday.

Not all was doom and gloom in the nineteenth century. Despite its having been berated in several previous publications for being a century in which originality and needle skills were sadly lacking, many highly decorative and intricately worked samplers were produced during the nineteenth century. 'The Little Florist', worked by Margaret Corin at Mrs Tumbath's Seminary in Penzance in 1833, has no morbid verse or rows of uniform alphabets but is instead a riot of colour and a highly decorative sampler. The accusation that the variety of stitches used in sampler making was decreasing is not in evidence in either Margaret Corin's sampler or in Ann Burnet's

A register of the children of John and Alice Chorlton, recording their births and deaths. This sampler, worked by Sarah when she was eighteen, reminds us that for most children in the late eighteenth and early nineteenth centuries, death was an ever-present reality.

This charming and highly decorative sampler by Margaret Corin was worked at Mrs Tumbath's seminary for young ladies in 1833. It is likely that plain sewing was taught separately, and for decorative needlework there was an additional fee to pay. (It was common to charge extra for 'fancy work' at these privately run schools.)

A charming depiction of rural life worked by Ann Burnet at Miss Gregson's seminary in Appleby, Westmorland, in 1838.

sampler worked at Miss Gregson's Seminary in 1828. In both samplers a wide variety of stitches has been chosen, and both works are imbued with a sense of freedom and joy, the girls coming from families affluent enough to send them to a private school.

The depiction of buildings on samplers became far more common during the nineteenth century, although they are certainly not unknown on eighteenth-century examples. Samplers worked with images of houses both humble and grand were particularly popular during the first half of the nineteenth century, and sometimes it has been concluded that the houses depicted are those of the 'workers'. In general it would seem that this is not the case, rather that the majority were either taken from printed sources – as seems probable in the case of Mary Goodger's sampler – or were simply based on house designs passed from teacher to pupil or schoolgirl to schoolgirl.

The charming sampler worked by Ann Hillman in 1806 depicts the life of a family of the leisured class placed in the garden of a large country home. It would seem reasonable to assume that this idyllic scene is illustrating Ann's own family

A typical early nineteenth-century house sampler worked by twelve-year-old Jane Gilbert. It is interesting that she has incorporated her family register in this sampler, recording the births of her parents and her siblings. Jane was one of nine children, a common size for a family at this date.

life; however, the existence of an almost identical sampler worked in the same year (Goodhart Collection, Montacute House, Somerset) indicates that this sampler is probably the result of the teaching of either a single governess or more likely the proprietor of a small privately run school for the daughters of the middle classes. Whether this design is the product of her imagination or comes from a printed source remains a mystery.[51]

Certainly the themes of family life occur frequently in the samplers of the nineteenth century, and so it is perhaps unsurprising that the house as the centre of family life should be a popular subject on the samplers worked. Houses were of course not the only buildings to appear on samplers, and many public buildings

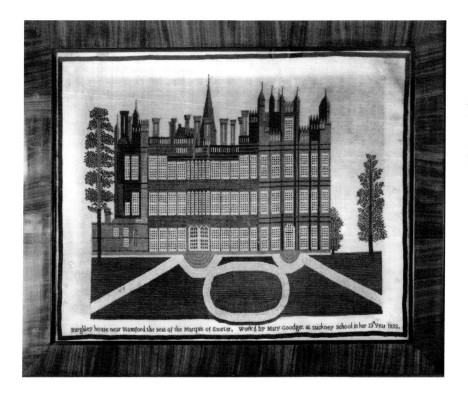

This rendition of Burghley House in Lincolnshire is almost certainly worked from a printed source. It is possible that the same source was used to draw the design on the ground and then worked by the whole class.

provided the main subject for nineteenth-century samplers. The sampler of Manchester Infirmary worked by Betty Ashworth and finished in 1828 provides us with one such example. Manchester Infirmary, founded in 1752 in a rented house on Shude Hill, had moved to the purpose built hospital depicted on the sampler in 1755. During the eighteenth century Manchester had grown at a tremendous rate, and the urban development and great public buildings erected in the new industrial

This sampler worked by Betty Ashworth in 1828 is typical of the depictions of large public buildings, which were popular subjects on nineteenth-century samplers.

centres such as Manchester were the subject of a great deal of civic and regional pride. Many engravings of these new public buildings were produced during the late eighteenth and early part of the nineteenth century, and it does not seem unreasonable to assume that the young Betty worked her sampler from just such a printed source.

In Scotland the working of houses and buildings was also very popular on nineteenth-century samplers. Margaret Kerr's depiction of a castle or large country house worked at Stewarton Schoolhouse in 1844 is one such example of the genre and again is likely to have been taken from a contemporary engraving. More commonly found on Scottish samplers is a standardised

The striking building depicted on Margaret's sampler is probably worked from a printed source. Margaret's mother is listed as a widowed washerwoman, and Margaret found employment as a bonnet knitter.

representation of a schoolhouse, often worked with a central, steeply pitched gable flanked on either side by a small wing, with the roof usually being worked in blue. It is worthy of note that on many Scottish house samplers the repeated use of the same patterns for the house is in evidence, making Scottish house samplers immediately recognisable and relatively easy to distinguish from those worked in England. The sampler worked by Margaret Holmes in 1841 is typical of the villa design worked on many Scottish samplers of the period. The earliest Scottish house pattern to appear, sometimes on samplers dating from the eighteenth century, is a tall building with a three-pointed roof, although on some, the central pitch has been flattened. The inclusion of a man standing on the front steps makes this type easily identified. The working of a front lawn often enclosed by a low brick wall and green and white fence is another indication of the sampler being Scottish,

Scottish house sampler depicting a small villa and similar in style to many worked in Scotland.

The sampler worked by Janet Anderson under the tuition of Mrs Huit has the typical front lawn surrounded by the same fence design seen on many Scottish samplers of the period.

as are the technique of working the lawn in three shades of chenille thread and the inclusion of round balls on top of the fence and gate posts.[52]

The inclusion of the band of flower heads with the twisted stem worked across the middle of the sampler by Jean Maxwell is typical of Scottish samplers. The design is reminiscent of the bands worked on seventeenth-century band samplers, but it is one which had ceased to be popular on English samplers of the period. This sampler also demonstrates the Scottish practice of including numerous pairs of initials, often relating to family members, and it is often possible to identify the initials of deceased relatives by their working in black thread. This sampler, in common with many whose origin is Scottish, is worked primarily in green and red silks, with the large pairs of initials in the two top corners of the sampler worked in typical Scottish lettering. The initials are most likely to be those of Jean's parents.

The sampler worked by Elizabeth Eiston in 1806 has a typical large Scottish house as its central image. The front lawn worked in chenille is also typical of Scottish samplers.

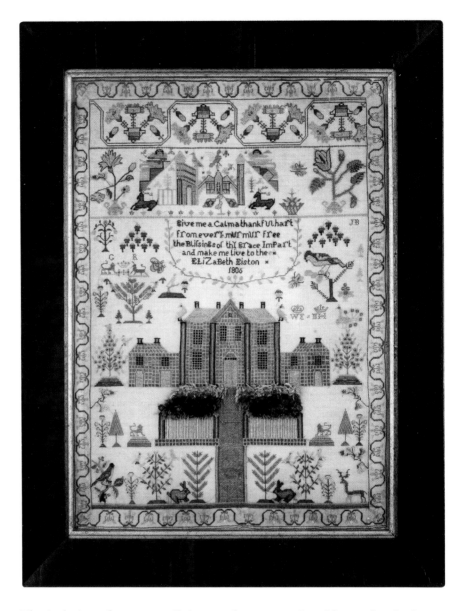

The inclusion of an open-tailed peacock on many Scottish samplers is also an indication of its origin.

The nineteenth century was to see the emergence of an increasing number of magazines specifically aimed at women and young girls. The sampler by Minnie Webber was worked as part of a competition sponsored by one such magazine, *The Girl's Own Paper*. The first edition was published in 1880 as a counterpart to *The Boy's Own Paper*, which had been founded some years earlier and had proved highly successful in both Britain and America. The magazine was aimed at working- and middle-class girls in their teens and young women in their twenties, and contained practical advice on housework, cookery, sewing, education, recreation, music, foreign countries and literature. The magazine was founded by the Religious Tract

Jean Maxwell has worked her sampler in the typical Scottish colour combination of red and green. The presence of two sets of initials worked in the two top corners is typical of Scottish work.

Society and it aimed to reinforce the moral well-being of its readership and maintain the cherished Victorian ideals of womanhood. The magazine ran several competitions for the working of samplers, with the rules of 'The New Sampler Competition' (entered by Minnie Webber) being announced in the May of 1882 and the results being announced in the following November. The rules of the competitions included detailed instructions as to the size, materials and the precise techniques to be included in the samplers entered. Each competition was divided into different age groups with prizes being awarded in each. A first prize of one guinea was awarded to the winner of each division with a prize of half a guinea awarded for the second place. First, second, and third class certificates were awarded to the girls who achieved the required number of marks for each discipline as outlined in the rules.

Interestingly, in the results of the darning sampler competition announced in another issue of the magazine, special praise is given to the work sent in by pupils attending the 'Orphan Working School':

> The authorities of the Orphan Working School are to be especially
> congratulated on the excellent teaching and training which are manifested

in the work of their scholars. The younger girls from this school show a very high standard of advancement for their age.[53]

Between about 1820 and 1870 the fashion for the delicate floral embroidery worked on muslin known as 'Ayrshire work' was flourishing. Ayrshire work developed when the newly widowed Lady Montgomerie of Eglington Castle returned to her Scottish estate from a trip to the Continent in 1814, bringing with her a baby's robe embroidered in France. The garment was seen by a Mrs Jamieson, an accomplished needlewoman and wife of an Ayrshire cotton merchant, who used the baby's robe to develop a distinctive style of embroidery, and she added more lace filling stitches to the designs she saw on the French worked robe. This was then taught to local women who were employed as out-workers, providing a much needed source of additional income for the families. The standard of embroidery demanded was very high, with poor workmanship rejected.

The demand for this type of work came from the clothing industry to decorate the ladies' clothes, the cuffs, collars and frills on men's shirts, handkerchiefs, caps, and baby clothes, particularly christening robes, in the most fashionable manner of the time. Although the work was named Ayrshire work after the area in Scotland where most of it was produced it was also made in other areas of Scotland and Ireland. Many items were made to individual orders; estimates vary, but between 80,000 and 400,000 women were employed in their own homes at the height of its production. The finished embroidery was collected by agents who would pay for the work, which would then be returned to the manufacturer to be made up into the finished item of clothing, washed and packed. A female worker embroidering Ayrshire work earned roughly the same wages as a bobbin lace maker in Devon. This type of work sold all over the world, and was particularly popular in North America.

Ayrshire embroidery involved stitching white cotton thread usually in satin or stem stitch onto white muslin with some spaces cut out and filled with needle lace. More than one worker would have been involved in the embroidering of any one completed design, one worker creating the design in the satin and stem stitch with the second worker working the lace in-fill. The wages of the workers was determined by their skill level: the workers specialising in the fine lace in-filling earned the higher wages. Ayrshire work was usually worked in hand, with a frame or hoop only being used for working the lace in-fills. The designs included a wide variety of naturalistic floral patterns, the fashion for which was influenced by the imported printed cottons from India which were so popular at the time. The designs were created by professional male embroiderers and transferred to

Minnie Webber won one guinea for her carefully worked plain sewing sampler. The prize mark is stamped onto the surface of the sampler in black ink.

Anonymous nineteenth-century Ayrshire work sampler.

the muslin or cotton ground initially by wooden stamps and from the late 1830s by a lithographic print. Commercial samplers were worked to be distributed to the out-workers for them to follow the designs, and whilst many samplers must have been produced, relatively few survive today. The example illustrated is one of the rare survivals of this industry.

This style of embroidery began to decline during the American Civil War (1861–5) when the northern states blockaded the southern states, preventing the export of cotton to Britain. The change in women's fashion further damaged the industry, with a decline in the popularity of fine floral embroidery, but the final demise came with the introduction of embroidery machines, particularly those used by Swiss manufacturers, which could produce the same style of embroidery at much cheaper prices than the hand work produced by the Scottish workers.[54]

Throughout the reign of Queen Victoria the fashion for Berlin work eclipsed almost all other forms of needlework. Berlin work was so named because the wools and patterns for the designs originated in Berlin. The first designs were published in 1804 by a Berlin print seller called Philipson, although Berlin work did not become popular until the 1830s when the designs were published in large numbers in London.

The first Berlin wool work patterns were printed in black and white on paper and then hand coloured. The embroiderer was then expected to draw the outline of the

design on to the ground cloth and stitch following the colours on the pattern. The publishers soon developed the patterns, printing the counted coloured charts onto graph paper, making it easier for the embroiderer, who no longer had to translate the patterns into wool colours. Most were sold as single sheets, which made them affordable. The printed patterns were exported to England and America in vast numbers, fuelling the craze for working a vast array of decorative objects. In Britain the craze was further fuelled by the Great Exhibition of 1851 and by the advent of ladies' magazines such as *The Englishwoman's Domestic Magazine*. The popularity of this type of work was undoubtedly increased by the increase in leisure time available to the growing number of middle-class women.

Technical innovation also played its part in the popularity of Berlin work. The huge advancement in dyeing processes which had taken place during the first half of the nineteenth century was followed in 1856 by the discovery of aniline dyes by an English chemist called William Henry Perkins. Perkins had accidentally discovered a lavender or purple dye made from aniline, a by-product of coal tar. The new colour was called mauve, and it caused great excitement in the British press. Berlin patterns made full use of this and other colours being produced by these new dyeing processes, and the softer wool threads now being spun took these more brilliant dyes exceptionally well.

Magazines published patterns for items such as seat covers, foot stools, slippers, purses, bell pulls and pincushions, together with instructions for their working and indications of the type of colours that should be used. Berlin work was often enhanced with silk threads, metal threads and beads and, possibly influenced by the Berlin patterns, beadwork itself saw a resurgence in popularity in the second half of the century. The influence of Berlin work can be seen on the sampler dated 20 October 1836 by M. A. Rendell (illustrated on page 2).

The detail taken from a long Berlin wool work sampler shows that the samplers were covered with Berlin patterns worked in small blocks, rather like the blocks of designs worked on the spot motif samplers of the seventeenth century. Unlike the early samplers, these samplers make no attempt to save space – rather they make a virtue of their length, some reaching over 10 feet in length. The patterns consist of floral and geometric motifs.

It is not believed that these samplers were the work of children but rather that they were worked by adults, either as reference sheets for professional embroiderers or to sell in needlework shops for amateurs to copy. These samplers usually contain a wide variety of different stitches, usually cross, tent, satin, Hungarian, Florentine and brick, and the samplers are usually bound at the edges with silk ribbon. Sometimes they have a piece of silk stitched to the top edge, intended to cover the sampler when rolled up.

It was the mechanisation of the late nineteenth century, the invention of the domestic sewing machine and the widespread availability of cheap manufactured clothing that was to contribute to the decline of the sampler.

Detail from a Berlin wool work sampler, probably dating from c.1860.

Opposite: This typically long Berlin work sampler is believed to be the work of an adult, possibly for display in a shop selling the materials necessary for doing Berlin work in the home.

In the early years of the twentieth century the outbreak of the First World War was to mark the beginnings of a decline in the widespread employment of domestic servants, and with it the gradual decline in the teaching of plain sewing to working-class girls. The daughters of the wealthy were to find the new diversions of the twentieth century rather more enticing than the appeal of decorative needlework.

During the twentieth and twenty-first centuries the working of samplers has become an increasingly popular recreational hobby or interest amongst adults. Numerous clubs, guilds and societies have formed throughout Europe and across America to teach the relevant stitches and techniques. A plethora of businesses have evolved to supply both the kits and materials necessary for the working of samplers, and there are many skilled professionals writing books, charting samplers for reproduction and teaching and offering advice on designing original samplers. The popularity of needlework as a modern day hobby provides something of a departure from the traditional reasons for the working of samplers and will provide a new chapter in the history and development of the sampler for study in the future. No doubt future historians and writers will document this development as part of the long and varied history of the sampler.

Chapter Six

THE AMERICAN CONNECTION

THE tradition of sampler making came to America from Europe, and because of the success of the early settlers from England it was the English tradition that was to be the biggest influence on the early development of American sampler making. There is little scope within the confines of this publication to deal with American samplers comprehensively; however, no study of British samplers would be complete without at least some discussion of the historical importance on the development of certain sampler-making traditions in America. To this end it is hoped that the examples discussed on these pages will serve to illustrate and give some background information explaining the connection between British and American sampler-making traditions.

The earliest permanent English settlement in colonial America was founded at Jamestown (originally the Jamestoune Setlyement) on 14 May 1610. The original settlers had left English shores in 1606 and landed on American soil in 1607, after deciding on the protection offered by the easy fortification and defence of an island in the James River. These early settlers (originally all men) were sponsored by the Virginia Company in England and were sent out to establish a colony for the profit of the company's investors. The first women came to the settlement in 1608 but men outnumbered women for most of the seventeenth century.

In 1620 the *Mayflower* set out from Southampton on its way to North Virginia, the colony founded by the Jamestown settlers. The passengers were mainly families fleeing persistent religious persecution and were searching for a land where they could practise their religion freely (they had been given permission to settle in Virginia). Bad weather forced the boat off course, and the passengers eventually landed north of their intended destination at Plymouth, Massachusetts.

For the early settlers, life was exceptionally hard and for the women many of the essentials of family life, including clothing and household furnishings, had to be made in the home. Imported textiles were scarce and, if available, they were beyond the means of most people. So whilst there was a great deal of hard manual labour for the women as well as the men, needlework was an essential skill. Since it was women who were responsible for working needlework it is not surprising that the earliest dated colonial samplers were worked in New England, where the earliest emigrant families settled, bringing with them their English traditions. The earliest known surviving colonial sampler was worked by Loara Standish, daughter of Myles Standish, who had travelled to America on the *Mayflower*. Although undated, the sampler was worked at some time around 1640 to 1650.

Once established in their new country, the Puritan leadership of New England established the cultural traditions of their homeland, and the educational practices

Opposite: Sampler worked by Susanna Russell in 1713. Note the almost identical arrangement of bands found on this sampler to the one worked in Philadelphia some twenty-three years later.

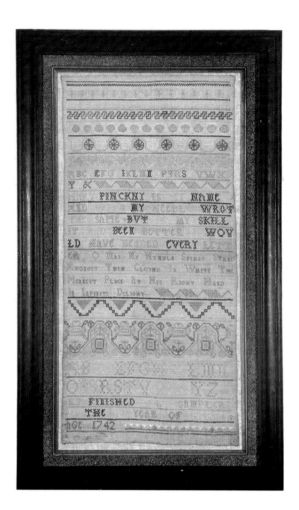

Typical eighteenth-century Boston sampler worked by Mary Pinckney in 1742.

with which they were familiar. Young children were first taught to read and spell and the girls taught to sew in small private schools, often run by a single master or mistress; indeed the early schools of Boston were often referred to as 'reading schools'.[55] The sampler worked by Loara Standish indicates that there was a teacher working in Plymouth at some time during the 1640s and that the foundation of schools had taken place relatively soon after the settlement was founded.

Of the samplers that were worked in the seventeenth century very few survive and, of those that do, there are none known to have been worked in either Virginia or the southern states.

In the early eighteenth century Boston had the largest urban population in colonial America, and it also had a sufficient number of schools to serve this population. It is noteworthy that the first important group of samplers to emerge from Boston, worked in the 1720s, are closely related to seventeenth-century English samplers both in form and design. The story of Adam and Eve seems to have been a favoured subject and continued to be so throughout the century. At this time the samplers of Philadelphia and Newport reflected the current English fashion of shortening the length of the sampler and enclosing the design with a border, so why many Boston samplers should take their inspiration from earlier English samplers remains a mystery. Young ladies were sent to Boston for their education from all over New England.

The population of the American colonies had grown enormously from just over 600,000 in 1700 to over 5 million in 1800. The growth was concentrated in the areas in or around Boston, Newport, New York, Philadelphia, and Charleston. Just as in Britain, growing prosperity and wealth amongst the middle classes was a catalyst for the demand and provision of a growing number of private schools and ladies' academies. The samplers worked in the early years of the eighteenth century are almost indistinguishable from their English counterparts, but later in the century a distinctive American style was to develop. The recognisable styles associated with the many individual schools (and teachers) that have been identified in colonial America tended to come from the major urban centres and most densely populated areas, where the demand for schooling was strongest and the necessary materials were available.

William Penn (1644–1718) landed in New Castle on the Delaware River in 1682 and took formal possession of the lands granted to him by Charles II. The land became known as Pennsylvania, and Philadelphia was soon established as its

This sampler is typical of those worked at school in Portland, Maine. Many samplers have been recorded from the same school, and they share the same colour palette and feature a large house with a white picket fence.

administrative heart. The city of brotherly love became known for its tolerance, a quality which led to the rapid growth and success of this colony. By 1730 Philadelphia was almost the same size as Boston, and it is from this city that one of the earliest known groups of samplers worked under the instruction of a named teacher comes. It is believed Elizabeth Marsh had emigrated to America from England in 1723. Elizabeth, who had been born in Worcestershire in 1683, already had four children by the time she emigrated, including her daughter Ann, born in 1714.

No immigration records of the family's journey exist but it has always been assumed that Elizabeth arrived in Philadelphia as an accomplished teacher; certainly she was employed to teach the daughters of some of Philadelphia's most prominent businessmen. James Logan had come to Pennsylvania as secretary to William Penn and had served as the family's attorney, as Mayor of Philadelphia (1723), and as Governor of Pennsylvania. We know from his household accounts and business ledger that Elizabeth was teaching his daughter Sarah Logan in 1727, although an earlier reference to her also exists, dated 1725: 'Elizabeth Marsh to acct of haberdashery £9 – 16 – 8¼.'

This sampler, worked under the instruction of Elizabeth and Ann Marsh by Mary Reeve in 1736, is typical of those worked in colonial Philadelphia. Elizabeth Marsh, Ann's mother, taught the children of many prominent Philadelphians.

In that same year Sarah worked a sampler, the earliest dated sampler attributed to the teaching of Elizabeth Marsh. The samplers worked under Elizabeth's instruction, including one worked by her daughter Ann, all show remarkable similarities of design, with the use of the same conventional floral border patterns and inscriptions. From 1727 the bands are enclosed within a border of Indian pinks.[57]

Very recently a sampler came to light which provides us with another chapter in the story of Elizabeth Marsh and the style of sampler which has come to be associated with both her and the city. The sampler by Susanna Russell, worked in 1713, shows a remarkable similarity to the samplers worked under the instruction of Elizabeth. Comparison of the border patterns used shows many which are identical in all but their working. Susanna's sampler predates Elizabeth's move to America by ten years. From genealogical research undertaken, a Susanna Russell whose dates would be commensurate with the working of this sampler has been located as living in Worcestershire, the same county in England from which Elizabeth came. Susanna was born in 1696, thirteen years after Elizabeth, and so would have been seventeen when she worked this sampler. Could it be that Elizabeth taught Susanna whilst in England or that both Elizabeth and Susanna attended the same school and so learnt the same sampler vocabulary, which Elizabeth then passed on to her pupils in America?

Despite a lack of formal teacher training many hundreds of women set up schools in America in the second half of the eighteenth century, most of them teaching out of necessity, being spinsters, widows or simply having to supplement the family income. The quality of these schools varied both in the abilities of the teacher and the subjects offered but one constant was the inclusion of needlework in the curriculum. Just as in England the standard of education a girl received was generally the result of the social and economic background from which she came. Whilst the majority of samplers were worked in school there is plenty of evidence that just as in England some samplers were worked within the home.

The American Revolution had been a very difficult time for the Quaker population of America, as their principle of pacifism had caused them to be seen as traitors to the cause of the freedom of the colonies. They had suffered politically, socially and economically, and were finding it increasingly difficult to preserve their values. Following the example of the London Monthly Meeting, the Philadelphia Monthly Meeting decided to found a school exclusively for Quaker children which would be dedicated to teaching Quaker beliefs. After a great many years of planning, discussion and fundraising, a parcel of land was purchased in Chester County and in 1799 Westtown School opened its doors for the first time to forty children. The location of the school was chosen to keep the children away from the temptations of the city and because the 600-acre site provided many of the materials necessary for building the school. Within a short space of time the school reached a population of two hundred, evenly divided between girls and boys.

Westtown became the most important Quaker school in America, and as such its teaching had much the same effect on the Quaker schools of America as that which Ackworth had on Quaker schools in England. The prominent American Quaker teacher and minister Rebecca Jones, who had sat on the Westtown committee, had travelled extensively throughout Britain and spent much of her time with many prominent English Quakers and advocates of female education, including Esther Tuke. Rebecca certainly visited Ackworth, in fact returning to America with a sampler worked by Ackworth scholar Candia Powers. Much impressed by Ackworth, the committee decided that Westtown would be set up on the same lines; even the plans for the buildings were based on those in Yorkshire.

It is perhaps little wonder then that the samplers worked at Westtown follow many of the same conventions as those worked at Ackworth. It has for example often been written that the motif of the bell flower is typical of American samplers. However, as we can see from Ann Hancock's sampler worked at Ackworth, this motif was being worked in England a full ten years before Westtown was even founded. The transference of styles of sampler making across the Atlantic is perhaps at its most marked on those worked by Quakers. Westtown influenced the foundation of numerous Quaker schools throughout America with many of its former scholars going on to teach and set up other Quaker schools. Note the

similarity between the vine leaf border on the sampler worked by Eliza Hoopes and on the unfinished extract sampler, both worked at Quaker schools in America, and the vine leaf border surrounding the inscription of Jane Leaver's name on her sampler of 1825, worked in England. It is interesting to note that on the unfinished extract sampler the vine leaf border was completed before the verse was worked.

The two smaller samplers worked by Eliza Payne in 1824 are in all respects typical of those worked in England around the same time, and without the existence of the third larger sampler worked in 1821 it would not even be obvious that there was a Quaker

Extract sampler worked by Eliza Hoopes under Quaker tuition in Chester County, Pennsylvania. This sampler shares an almost identical border with the unfinished extract probably worked at Westtown School. The Hoopes' house is still standing.

Unfinished Quaker extract sampler. This sampler was left unfinished in something of a hurry as a thread can still be seen hanging from the last letter worked.

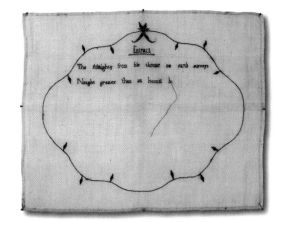

Jane Leaver's sampler worked in 1825 is surrounded with a vine leaf border and bell flowers, typical of Quaker instruction.

connection. Eliza Payne was born in Suffolk County, New York, and her work is typical of that worked at the Nine Partners School in Dutchess County, where it seems likely that the young Eliza was brought up (both her parents and grandparents had been born in that county). It is possible that Eliza either attended the Nine Partners School or alternatively one of the small privately run schools in the area. Many of the medallions worked on Eliza's sampler of 1821 are identical to those worked on the Ackworth medallion samplers. As yet no definitive evidence has emerged to explain how these motifs were transferred from one side of the Atlantic to the other – was it from a pattern or copy book, or was it taken to America with a teacher who had attended an English Quaker school? To date, no copy or pattern book containing medallions has been found.[58]

Left: Pair of small samplers worked by Eliza Payne. These samplers were probably worked at a Quaker institution in Dutchess County, New York State, possibly at the Nine Partners School.

Below: This sampler worked by Eliza Payne is worked with a half medallion border typical of the Nine Partners School. Without this bordered sampler it would have been very difficult to have identified these samplers as having been taught under Quaker instruction.

The second half of the eighteenth century was one of enormous political change in America; the War of Independence marked a move away from the influence that Britain was to hold over America. Early in the colonies' history the middle classes had relied on imported goods to satisfy the demand for the decorative arts (imported items were often seen as being superior), but as dissatisfaction with the rule from England spread the colonists looked more to their own craftsmen to satisfy their demand. This independence is reflected in the samplers worked in America in the third quarter of the century, with many teachers developing their own highly recognisable styles, which display many characteristics not seen on English samplers of the period.

Distinctive American sampler worked by Jane Bird in 1802 at school in Marblehead, Massachusetts.

The linen used in the working of early American samplers was generally spun locally as imported linen was very expensive due to the duty imposed on imported goods. As a result, the linen was often coarse in nature, and frequently unbleached. It is not unusual to find samplers worked on tan, light brown, green or even occasionally black linen grounds. Tammy or wool ground fabric was used far less than in Britain and tiffany was not used until the nineteenth century. The type of ground fabric used for sampler making can be a useful tool in identifying the origin of early samplers worked in America.

Just as in Britain the primary thread used for the stitching of samplers was silk, but occasionally wool thread or linen was used. After independence, America started to import more of its goods directly, and silk thread and silk fabric became much more accessible and less expensive. Just as in England needlework samplers consisted of both plain sewing types and the very decorative embroidered samplers worked at the small private academies, where the subjects offered to the daughters of the middle classes were very similar to those offered to the daughters of the English middle classes. Indeed there are countless adverts placed by teachers in the major cities declaring themselves newly arrived from England.

This sampler, wrought by Martha C. Hooton and dated 1827, forms part of a highly recognisable group of samplers worked in Burlington County, New Jersey, during the first half of the nineteenth century.

On 20 May 1765 the *New York Mercury* carried the following advert:

> Mary Bosworth, Lately from London, takes this method to inform the public,
>
> That she has opened a school in Cortland street, near Mr John Lary's; wherein she teaches young masters and misses to read and learn them all sorts of verse; She likewise learns young ladies plain work, samplairs…[59]

In the late eighteenth and early nineteenth centuries many of the surviving American decorative samplers display the symbols associated with their liberty and the new republic. The eagle on the larger Payne sampler is for example a motif frequently seen on American samplers. American samplers from the later part of the eighteenth and throughout the nineteenth century often display more freedom and less symmetry than their English counterparts. In recent years a great deal of work has been done to identify the teachers behind American schoolgirl needlework and many schools have been identified and distinctive styles attributed to these schools.[60]

FOOTNOTES

Introduction

1. A. F. Kendrick. *Catalogue of Samplers – Victoria and Albert Museum*. 3rd edition, 1921, page 2.

2. A. F. Kendrick. *Catalogue of Samplers – Victoria and Albert Museum*. 3rd edition, 1921, page 3.

Chapter 1: The Seventeenth Century

3. Eileen J. Bennett. *Jane Bostocke…..the rest of the story*. The Sampler House, 2004.

4. Kathleen Staples. 'Embroidered Furnishings: Questions of Production and Usage'. *English Embroidery from the Metropolitan Museum of Art 1580–1700. Twixt Art and Nature.* Yale University Press, 2008, page 24.
   Moody, Joanna (editor). *The Private Life of an Elizabethan Lady: The Diary of Lady Margaret Hoby, 1599–1605*. Sutton Publishing, 1998. 'I wrought tell dinner time'; 'after dinner I went to worke'.

5. Kathleen Staples. 'Embroidered Furnishings: Questions of Production and Usage'. *English Embroidery from the Metropolitan Museum of Art 1580–1700. Twixt Art and Nature.* Yale University Press, 2008, page 29.

6. A. F. Kendrick. 'Embroideries at the Whitworth Art Gallery, Manchester'. *Connoisseur* 86, no. 351 (1930), pages 288–94 (page 289).

7. Frances N. Teague. *Bathsua Makin, Woman of Learning: Bathsua – Essay to Revive the Antient Education of Gentlewoman. 1673*. Published 1998.

8. Andrew Morrall and Melinda Watt. 'Embroidery and Education'. *English Embroidery from the Metropolitan Museum of Art 1580–1700. Twixt Art and Nature.* Yale University Press, 2008, page 145.

9. Edwina Ehrman. *The Judith Hayle Samplers*. Needleprint, 2007.

10. Bromiley Phelan, Dorothy; Hansson, Eva-Lotta; Holdsworth, Jacqueline. *The Goodhart Samplers*. Needleprint, 2008.
    Spot motif sampler MON/G/005 page 25, dated 1640. MON/G/013 page 54, dated 1657. MON/G/044 p60, dated 1674, initialled MS. MON/G/011 page 62, dated 1651, Elizabeth Bee. MON/G/036 page 70, dated 1670, Elizabeth Branch.

11. Averil Colby. *Samplers*. B.T. Batsford Ltd, 1964, page 22.

12. Richard Shorleyker. *A Schole-house for the Needle*. London, 1632.

13. John Parkinson. *Paradisi in sole paradisus terrestris*. London, 1629.
    Andrew Morrall. 'Regaining Eden: Representations of Nature in Seventeenth-Century English Embroidery.' *English Embroidery from the Metropolitan Museum of Art 1580–1700. Twixt Art and Nature.* Yale University Press, 2008, pages 79–97 (page 80).

14. Andrew Morrall. 'Regaining Eden: Representations of Nature in Seventeenth-Century English Embroidery.' *English Embroidery from the Metropolitan Museum of Art 1580–1700. Twixt Art and Nature.* Yale University Press, 2008, pages 79–97.

15. Mary E. Hazard. *Elizabethan Silent Language*. University of Nebraska Press, 2000, page 36. Quoted in *The Goodhart Samplers* MON/G/027, page 30.

16. Averil Colby. *Samplers*. B. T. Batsford Ltd, 1964, page 158.

17. Naomi Tarrant. 'Samplers made in Scotland'. *History Scotland*, May/June 2004, pages 28–34.

18. Michael Olmert. 'The Hospitable Pineapple'. Published in the winter 1997–8 edition of the Foundation Journal *Colonial Williamsburg*.

Chapter 2: The Eighteenth Century

19. G. A. Fothergill. *Notes on Scottish Samplers – Proceedings of the Society of Antiquaries of Scotland*, 8 March 1909, pages 180–205, page 185.

20. Joy Jarrett and Rebecca Scott. *Changing Styles – The Eighteenth Century, One Hundred Years of Sampler Making*. Witney Antiques, 2007. Catalogue no. 3.

21. Joy Jarrett and Rebecca Scott. *An Exceptional Endeavor – British Samplers and Historic Embroideries*. Witney Antiques, 2003. Catalogue no. 8, page 14.

22. Joy Jarrett and Rebecca Scott. *Samplers – Mapped and Charted*. Witney Antiques, 2005. 'A Note on Map Samplers', page 2.

Chapter 3: Quaker Samplers

23. The Life and Beliefs of George Fox and the Beginnings of Quakerism. http://encyclopedia.laborlawtalk.com/George_Fox. *George Fox. An Autobiography*. Edited with an introduction and notes by Rufus M. Jones.

24. Carol Humphrey. *Quaker School Girl Samplers from Ackworth*. Needleprint and Ackworth Estates, 2006.

25. Carol Humphrey. *Friends a Common Thread, Samplers with a Quaker Influence*. Witney Antiques, 2008, page 11.

26. List of Ackworth Scholars 1779–1879. Reprinted by Witney Antiques, 2006. See also Carol Humphrey. *Friends a Common Thread, Samplers with a Quaker Influence*. Witney Antiques, 2008, page 70.

27. W. K. and E. M. Sessions. 'The Tuke's of York'. Advertisement for Esther Tuke's School, York, 1784. Sessions, York, 1971.

28. Carol Humphrey. *Friends a Common Thread, Samplers with a Quaker Influence*. Witney Antiques, 2008.

29. Carol Humphrey. *Friends a Common Thread, Samplers with a Quaker Influence*. Witney Antiques, 2008, page 31.

30. Carol Humphrey. *Friends a Common Thread, Samplers with a Quaker Influence*. Witney Antiques, 2008, page 29.

Chapter 4: Samplers of the Poor

31. Rebecca Scott and Joy Jarrett. *Stitched in Adversity, Samplers of the Poor*. Witney Antiques, 2006. See Introduction.

32. Edwina Ehrman. *The Judith Hayle Samplers*. Needleprint, 2007, page 12. Suffolk Record Office, Ipswich, HA247/6/2-3 (Edgar Family Papers).

33. Carol Humphrey. *Fitzwilliam Museum Handbook*. Cambridge University Press, 1997. Catalogue no. 23, page 56.

34. Rebecca Scott and Joy Jarrett. *Stitched in Adversity, Samplers of the Poor.* Witney Antiques, 2006. See Catalogue nos. 23–6.

35. Mark K. Smith. *Hannah Moore: Sunday Schools, Education and Youth Work.* Encyclopaedia of Informal Education, 2002. http://www.infed.org/thinkers/more.htm.

36. Rebecca Scott and Joy Jarrett. *Stitched in Adversity, Samplers of the Poor.* Witney Antiques, 2006. Taken from *History of Cheltenham*, Griffith's, 1838.

37. 'The Bristol Miracle'. George Muller Foundation. For further information on the orphanage contact the George Muller Foundation: Muller House, 7 Gotham Park, Bristol BS6 6DA.

38. Michael Peters. *Robert Raikes: The Founder of Sunday School 1780.* Pleasant Word, 2008.

39. City of Manchester Archives Department. Sarah Trimmer. *An Address to Ladies concerning Sunday Schools; The Establishment of Schools of Industry etc.* First published 1787.

40. Thomas Swindells. *Manchester Streets and Manchester Men.* Published by subscription, 1908.

41. Frances M. Page. 'Christ's Hospital, Hertford', page 77.

42. Christopher Hawes. *Poor Relations – The Making of a Eurasian Community in British India 1773–1833.* Curzon Press, 1996, page 22.

43. Christopher Hawes. *Poor Relations – The Making of a Eurasian Community in British India 1773–1833.* Curzon Press, 1996, page 25. Public Letters from Bombay, 19 July 1815, 20 December, 1817, BC, F/4/503, no. 12032; F/4/561, no. 13788, IOR.

44. Christopher Hawes. *Poor Relations – The Making of a Eurasian Community in British India 1773–1833.* Curzon Press, 1996, page 26. *An Account of the Free School, Calcutta, and of Its Proceedings, Midsummer 1818.* St Thomas's.

45. Rebecca Scott and Joy Jarrett. *Stitched in Adversity, Samplers of the Poor.* Witney Antiques, 2006. Catalogue no. 15.

46. *Daily Chronicle,* 22 August 1885. 'Death of a Notorious Woman'.

47. Rebecca Quinton. *Patterns of Childhood, Samplers from Glasgow Museums.* The Herbert Press, 2005. Catalogue no. 51, page 77.

Chapter 5: The Nineteenth Century.

48. Ian D. Gilroy. *The Rev. Andrew Bell, Founder of Madras College.* Published by David Galloway, 1997.

49. William Corston. *A Brief Sketch of the Life of Joseph Lancaster.* 1840.

50. Verse taken from a sampler worked by Margaret Morgan, aged 14, at S. Westbrook's School, Wales, 1839. Anne Sebba. *Samplers: Five Centuries of a Gentle Craft.* Weidenfeld & Nicolson, London, 1979, page 124.

51. Bromiley Phelan, Dorothy; Hansson, Eva-Lotta; Holdsworth, Jacqueline. *The Goodhart Samplers.* Needleprint, 2008. MON/G/094, sampler by Elizabeth Tatham 1806.

52. Naomi Tarrant. 'Samplers made in Scotland'. *History Scotland,* May/June 2004, pages 28–34.

53. *The Girl's Own Paper*, vol. 4, no. 189, 11 August 1883 – Results of the prize competitions, page 711.

54. Margaret Swain. *Ayrshire and Other Whitework*. Shire Publications 1982.

Chapter 6: The American Connection

55. Ellwood P. Cubberley. *A History of Education*. Originally published in 1902. Reprinted by Kessinger Publishing Co., 2004, page 287.

56. Anne Sebba. *Samplers: Five Centuries of a Gentle Craft*. Weidenfeld & Nicolson, London, 1979, page 82.

57. Betty Ring. *Girlhood Embroidery*, vol. II. Alfred A. Knopf, New York, 1993, pages 330–7.

58. Carol Humphrey. *Friends a Common Thread, Samplers with a Quaker Influence*. Witney Antiques, 2008, pages 54–5.

59. For more information on school teachers in eighteenth- and nineteenth-century New York: Betty Ring. *Girlhood Embroidery*, 2 vols. Alfred A. Knopf, New York, 1993: 'Needlework of New York', pages 295–329.

60. For further reading on the many different known American teachers who taught sampler making, and who often had their own distinctive styles, refer to: Betty Ring. *Girlhood Embroidery*, 2 vols. Alfred A. Knopf, New York, 1993.

PLACES TO VISIT

UNITED KINGDOM

Embroiderers' Guild, Apt 41, Hampton Court Palace, Surrey KT8 9AU. Telephone: 0208 943 1229. Website: www.embroierersguild.org.uk

Fitzwilliam Museum, Trumpington Street, Cambridge CB2 1RB. Telephone: 01223 332900. Website: www.fitzmuseum.cam.ac.uk

Gawthorpe Hall, Padiham, near Burnley, Lancashire BB12 8UA. Telephone: 01282 771004. Website: www.nationaltrust.org.uk/main/w-gawthorpehall

Glasgow Museums, The Burrell Collection, Pollok Country Park, 2060 Pollokshaws Road, Glasgow G43 1AT. Telephone: 0141 287 2550. Website: www.glasgowmuseums.com

Hove Museum and Art Gallery, 19 New Church Road, Hove, East Sussex BN3 4AB. Telephone: 01273 290200. Website: www.hove.virtualmuseum.info

Lady Lever Art Gallery, Port Sunlight, Liverpool CH62 5EQ. Telephone: 0151 478 4136. Website: www.liverpoolmuseums.org.uk/ladyLever/

Manx Museum, Douglas, Isle of Man IM1 3LY. Telephone: 01624 648000. Website: www.gov.im/mnh/heritage/museums/manxmuseum.xml

Montacute House (The Goodhart Collection), Montacute, Somerset TA15 6XP. Telephone: 01935 823289. Website: www.nationaltrust.org.uk/main/w-montacute/

Museum of Costume and Textiles, 51 Castle Gate, Nottingham NG1 6AF. Telephone: 0115 915 3500.

Strangers' Hall Museum, Charing Cross, Norwich, Norfolk NR2 4AL. Telephone: 01603 667229. Website: www.museums.norfolk.gov.uk

Victoria and Albert Museum, Cromwell Road, South Kensington, London SW7 2RL. Telephone: 020 7942 2000. Website: www.vam.ac.uk

Whitby Museum, Pannett Park, Whitby, North Yorkshire YO21 1RE. Telephone: 01947 602908. Website: www.whitbymuseum.org.uk

Whitworth Art Gallery, University of Manchester, Oxford Road, Manchester M15 6ER. Telephone: 0161 275 7450. Website: www.whitworth.manchester.ac.uk

Witney Antiques, 96–100 Corn Street, Witney, Oxfordshire OX28 6BU. Telephone: 01993 703902. Website: www.witneyantiques.com

UNITED STATES OF AMERICA

Cooper Hewitt, National Design Museum, The Smithsonian Institution, New York. Website: www.cooperhewitt.org

De Witt Wallace Decorative Arts Museum, Colonial Williamsburg Foundation, Williamsburg, Virginia. Website: www.history.org/history/museums/dewitt_gallery.cfm

Los Angeles County Museum of Art, Los Angeles. Website: www.lacma.org

The Metropolitan Museum of Art, New York. Website: www.metmuseum.org
Museum of Fine Arts, Boston. Website: www.mfa.org
Philadelphia Museum of Art, Philadelphia. Website: www.philamuseum.org
Winterthur Museum and Country Estate, Winterthur, Delaware. Website:
   www.winterthur.org

A sampler by Lucy Walton, 1831

FURTHER READING

Arthur, Liz. *Embroidery 1600–1700 at the Burrell Collection.* John Murray, 1995.

Bolton, Ethel Stanwood, and Coe, Eva Johnston. *American Samplers.* Dover Publications, 1973.

Bromiley Phelan, Dorothy; Hansson, Eva-Lotta; and Holdsworth, Jacqueline. *The Goodhart Samplers.* Needleprint, 2008.

Brooke, Xanthe. *The Lady Lever Art Gallery Catalogue of Embroideries.* National Museums and Galleries on Merseyside, 1992.

Browne, Claire, and Wearden, Jennifer. *Samplers from the Victoria & Albert Museum.* V&A Publications, 1999.

Clabburn, Pamela. *Samplers.* Second edition, Shire Publications, 1998.

Colby, Averil. *Samplers.* B. T. Batsford, 1964.

Ehrman, Edwina. *The Judith Hayle Samplers.* Needleprint, 2007.

Huish, Marcus B. *Samplers and Tapestry Embroideries.* London, 1913.

Humphrey, Carol. *Friends a Common Thread, Samplers with a Quaker Influence.* Witney Antiques, 2008.

Humphrey, Carol. *Quaker Samplers from Ackworth.* Needleprint, 2006.

Humphrey, Carol. *Samplers. Fitzwilliam Museum Handbook.* Cambridge University Press, 1997.

Quinton, Rebecca. *Patterns of Childhood – Samplers from Glasgow Museums.* The Herbert Press in association with Glasgow City Council, 2005.

Ring, Betty. *Girlhood Embroidery.* 2 volumes, Alfred A. Knopf, 1993.

Sebba, Anne. *Samplers: Five Centuries of a Gentle Craft.* Thames & Hudson, 1979.

Swan, Susan Burrows. *Plain and Fancy: American Women and their Needlework 1700–1850.* Holt Rinehart & Winston, 1977.

Synge, Lanto. *The Royal School of Needlework Book of Needlework and Embroidery.* Collins, 1986.

Synge, Lanto. *Art of Embroidery: History of Style and Technique.* Antique Collectors' Club, 2001.

Tarrant, Naomi. *Textile Treasures: An Introduction to European Decorative Textiles for Home and Church in the NMS.* National Museums of Scotland Publishing, 2001.

Witney Antiques. *Upstairs Downstairs Plain and Fancy.* Witney Antiques, 1999.

Witney Antiques. *Samplers: Mapped and Charted.* Witney Antiques, 2005.

Witney Antiques. *Stitched in Adversity – Samplers of the Poor.* Witney Antiques, 2006.

INDEX